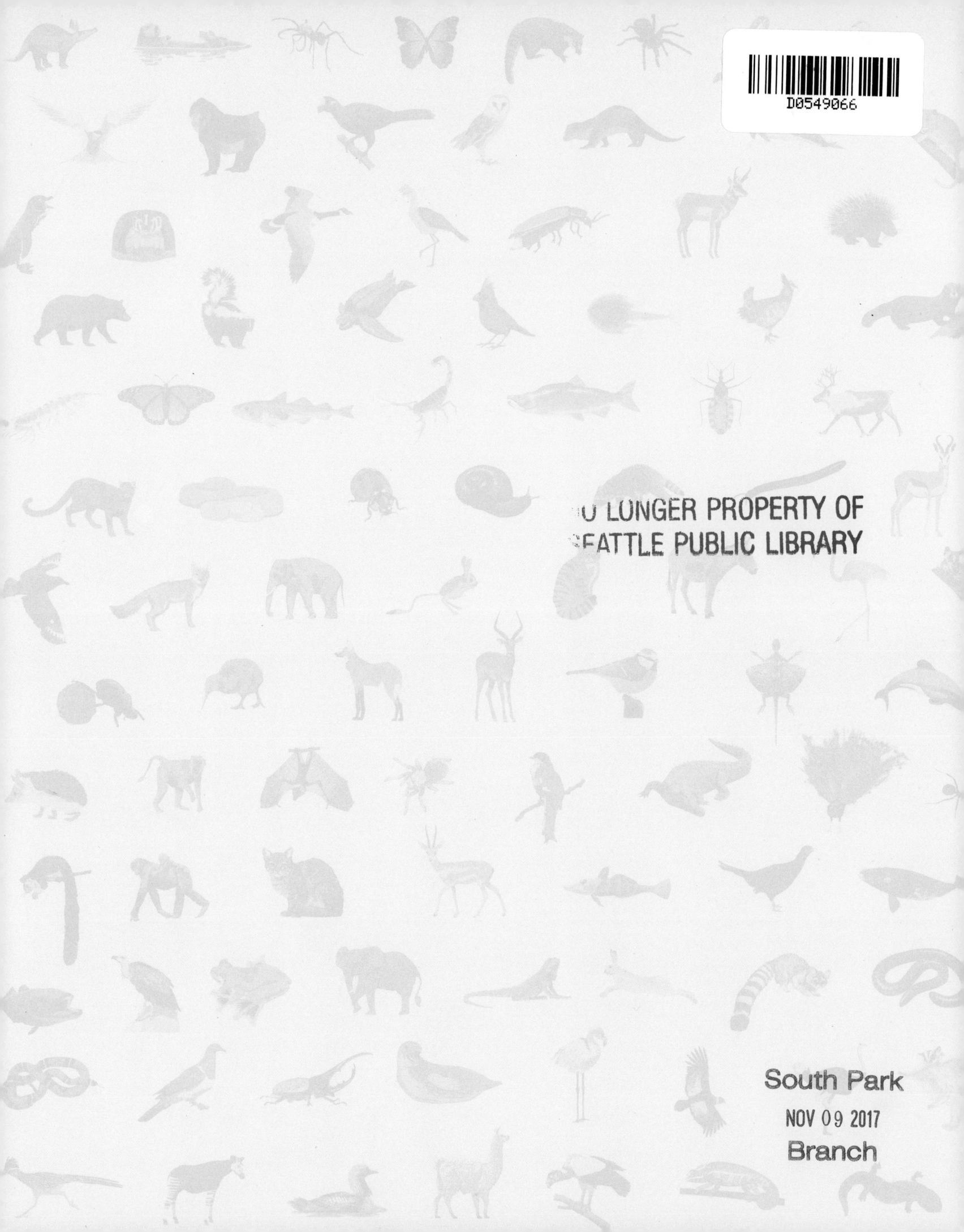

D0549066

O LONGER PROPERTY OF
SEATTLE PUBLIC LIBRARY

South Park
NOV 09 2017
Branch

SMITHSONIAN

Children's Illustrated Animal ATLAS

DK | Penguin Random House

Author Jamie Ambrose
Editor Olivia Stanford
Project editor Allison Singer
Project art editor Hoa Luc
Designer Rhea Gaughan
US Senior editor Shannon Beatty
US editor Jane Perlmutter

Map illustrator Jeongeun Park
Cartography Ed Merritt, Simon Mumford
Illustrators Maltings Partnership, Molly Lattin, Bettina Myklebust Stovne, Oliver Magee
Additional design Lucy Sims, Yamini Panwar
Assistant editor Prerna Grewal
Jacket coordinator Francesca Young
Jacket designer Hoa Luc
Managing editor Laura Gilbert
Managing art editor Diane Peyton Jones
Pre-production producer Nikoleta Parasaki
Producer Niamh Tierney
Art director Martin Wilson
Publisher Sarah Larter
Publishing director Sophie Mitchell

First American Edition, 2017
Published in the United States by DK Publishing
345 Hudson Street, New York, New York 10014

Copyright © 2017 Dorling Kindersley Limited.
DK, a Division of Penguin Random House LLC
17 18 19 20 21 10 9 8 7 6 5 4 3 2 1
001-298819-Aug/2017

All rights reserved.
Without limiting the rights under the copyright reserved above, no part of this publication may be reproduced, stored in or introduced into a retrieval system, or transmitted, in any form, or by any means (electronic, mechanical, photocopying, recording, or otherwise), without the prior written permission of the copyright owner.
Published in Great Britain by Dorling Kindersley Limited.

A catalog record for this book is available from the Library of Congress.

DK books are available at special discounts when purchased in bulk for sales promotions, premiums, fund-raising, or educational use. For details, contact: DK Publishing Special Markets, 345 Hudson Street, New York, New York 10014 SpecialSales@dk.com

ISBN: 978-1-4654-6203-9

Printed and bound in Hong Kong

A WORLD OF IDEAS:
SEE ALL THERE IS TO KNOW

Contents

4 How to use this book
6 The world

8 North America
10 North American taiga
12 Great Plains
13 Eastern forests
14 Western deserts
16 Central America
17 Caribbean
18 Florida Everglades

20 South America
22 Amazon rain forest
24 Andean mountains
26 Temperate pampas
28 Pantanal
29 Galápagos
30 Cerrado
32 Cordillera Blanca

34 Africa
36 Sahara desert
38 Congo Basin
40 Southern savanna

42 Kalahari desert
43 Madagascar
44 Kruger National Park

46 Europe

48 Northern European taiga
50 British Isles
52 European forests
54 The Alps
55 European steppe
56 Mediterranean scrubland
58 Białowieża Forest

60 Asia

62 Russian taiga
64 Asian steppe
65 Central Asian deserts
66 Tibetan Plateau
68 East Asian forests
70 Arabian Peninsula
71 Indian forests
72 Southeast Asian rain forest
74 Gobi desert

76 Australasia

78 Australia
80 New Zealand
82 Great Barrier Reef

84 Antarctica
86 The Arctic
88 Oceans and seas

90 Atlas picture quiz
92 Glossary
93 Index
96 Credits

Smithsonian

This trademark is owned by the Smithsonian Institution and is registered in the U.S Patent and Trademark Office.

Consultant Dr. Don E. Wilson, Curator Emeritus, Department of Vertebrate Zoology, National Museum of Natural History, Smithsonian

Smithsonian Enterprises
Product Development Manager Kealy Gordon
Licensing Manager Ellen Nanney
Vice President, Consumer and Education Products Brigid Ferraro
Senior Vice President, Consumer and Education Products Carol LeBlanc
President Christopher A. Liedel

Established in 1846, the Smithsonian Institution—the world's largest museum and research complex—includes 19 museums and galleries and the National Zoological Park. The total number of objects, works of art, and specimens in the Smithsonian's collection is estimated at 154 million. The Smithsonian is a renowned research center, dedicated to public education, national service, and scholarship in the arts, sciences, and history.

How to use this book

An atlas usually shows maps of different countries, but animals often live across borders. The maps in this book show many of the world's different habitats, which is the environment where an animal lives, such as a desert. Some islands are also shown, since they have animals that are found nowhere else.

Compass
The compass always points north (N) in line with the map. It also shows the direction of south (S), east (E), and west (W).

Animal pictures
Pictures with descriptions pick out particular animals that live in an area.

Independent states
Small independent states, such as Monaco, are shown with a red border and a solid red dot, and the name is in capital letters.

Rivers
Each country's largest rivers are shown as continuous blue lines.

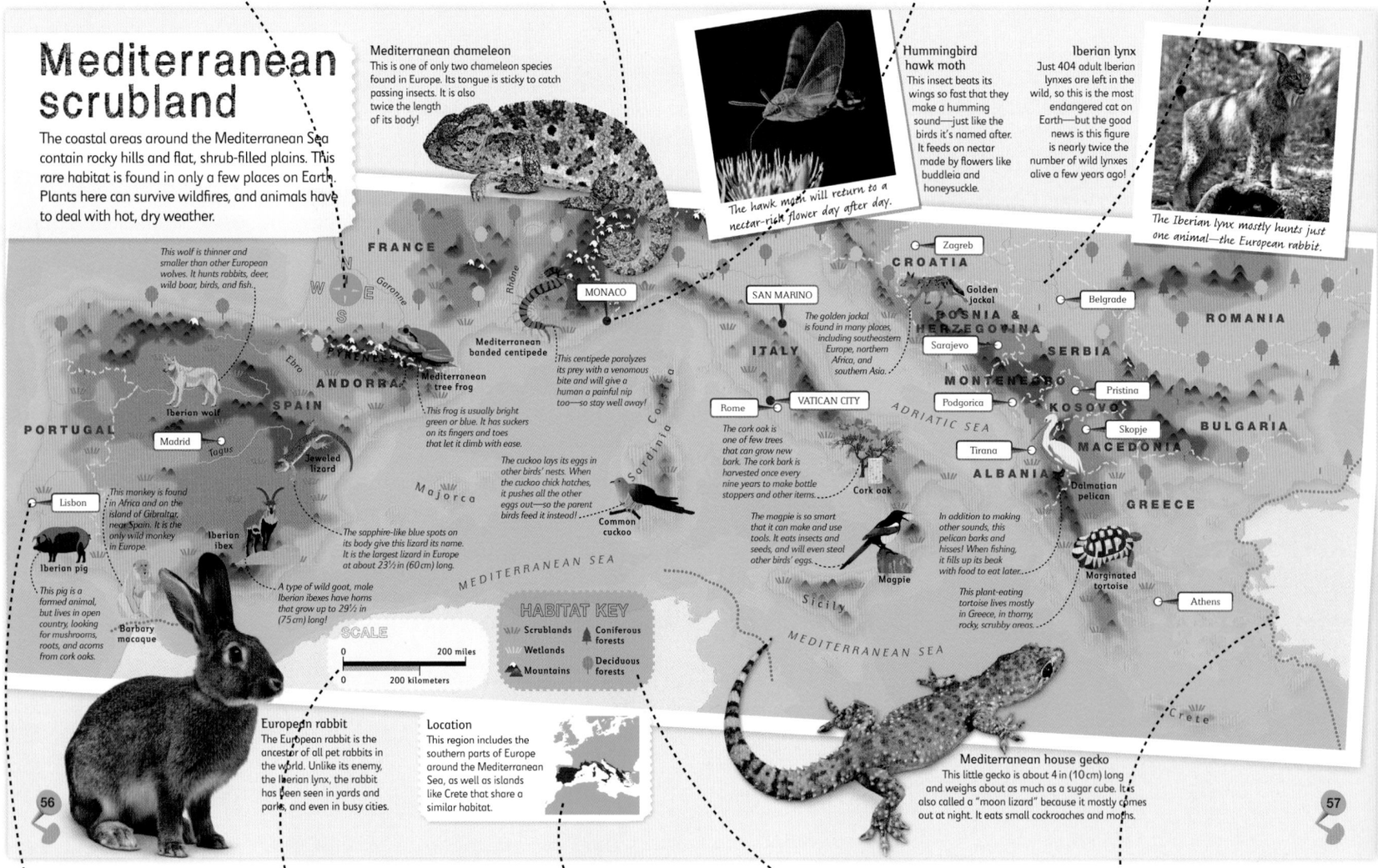

Capital
A country's capital city is marked with a red outline. Some countries have more than one capital city.

Scale
The scale shows the size of the areas and the distances between different points on the map.

Location
The location box shows you where each area is found in relation to the land around it.

Habitat key
Every map has a key that lists the types of habitats found in that area.

Bordering continents
Around the edges of some maps you can see parts of bordering continents in a cream color.

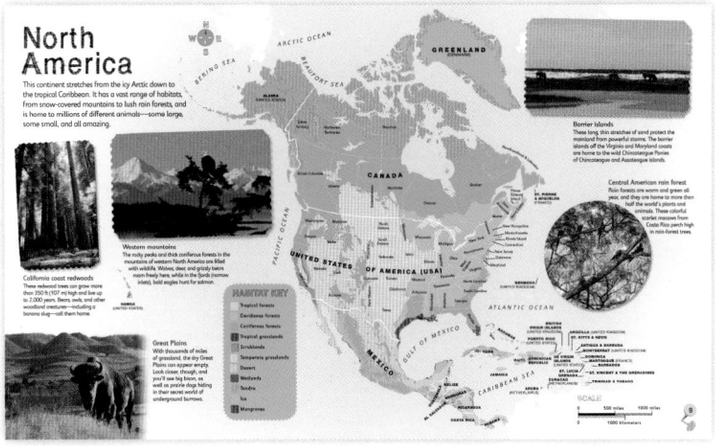

Continent maps

The continent maps are colored to show the biomes found on each continent. A biome is a large area of one type of habitat, and the animals and plants in it. Photographs show some of the places in these biomes.

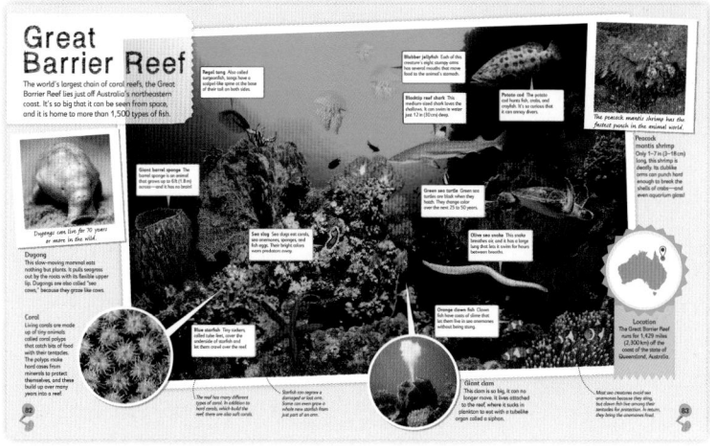

Feature habitats

The feature spreads show a specific place and some of the animals that live there. In reality, not all the animals would be found together at the same time, since they are awake at different times of day, and would often avoid each other to prevent being eaten!

Habitats

These symbols show the different types of habitat on each map.

Mountains
High, rugged mountainous areas are often covered with snow.

Coniferous forests
Trees in coniferous forests usually have needlelike leaves that are kept all year round.

Wetlands
Wetlands are marshy, swampy areas, such as the Pantanal in Brazil.

Hot desert
Hot deserts, such as the Sahara, are dry, sandy areas. Few plants grow here.

Oceans and seas
Huge stretches of water are found around the Earth's seven continents.

Mangroves
Mangrove trees grow on coasts in salty water. Their long roots stick out of the water.

Temperate grasslands
Flat, grassy plains with few trees found in seasonal areas are temperate grasslands, such as prairie, steppe, and pampas.

Cold desert
Cold deserts, such as the Gobi, are cold, dry stretches of land.

Tropical forests
Rain forests, such as the Amazon, get a lot of rain and heat so the trees grow very tall.

Coral reefs
Coral reefs grow in shallow waters. They are built by coral animals.

Tropical grasslands
Flat, grassy plains with few trees found in hot areas are tropical grasslands, such as savanna and cerrado.

Snow and ice
Frozen areas are found high up in the mountains and at the North and South Poles.

Deciduous forests
Trees in deciduous forests usually have broad leaves that are lost in the fall, or during the dry season.

Scrublands
Low-lying plants and grasses grow in scrubland areas with small trees, such as in southern Spain.

Borders

Borders show how the Earth's land is divided into countries.

Country borders
The borders between countries are shown with a broken white line.

Disputed borders
Some countries disagree about where the border between them should be. These borders are shown with a white dotted line.

Continent borders
A broken orange line shows where the border is between two continents.

The world

The types of habitats found on each of the Earth's seven continents depends on the usual weather, or climate, of an area. Five invisible lines divide the world into three climatic zones: the tropical zone is hot, the temperate zones are seasonal, and the polar zones are cold.

ARCTIC OCEAN
Polar zone
Inside the polar circles, around the North and South Poles, it is dry and very cold.
EUROPE
ASIA
Temperate zone
Both temperate zones have warm summers and cold winters. Forests in the temperate zone often lose their leaves in the fall or during the dry season.
PACIFIC OCEAN
Tropical zone
The area between the tropics, around the equator, is very hot. Most rain forests are found in this zone.
INDIAN OCEAN
AUSTRALASIA
Temperate zone
SOUTHERN OCEAN
ANTARCTICA
Polar zone

North America

This continent stretches from the icy Arctic down to the tropical Caribbean. It has a vast range of habitats, from snow-covered mountains to lush rain forests, and is home to millions of different animals—some large, some small, and all amazing.

California coast redwoods

These redwood trees can grow more than 350 ft (107 m) high and live up to 2,000 years. Bears, owls, and other woodland creatures—including a banana slug—call them home.

Western mountains

The rocky peaks and thick coniferous forests in the mountains of western North America are filled with wildlife. Wolves, deer, and grizzly bears roam freely here, while in the fjords (narrow inlets), bald eagles hunt for salmon.

Great Plains

With thousands of miles of grassland, the dry Great Plains can appear empty. Look closer, though, and you'll see big bison, as well as prairie dogs hiding in their secret world of underground burrows.

N
W E
S

ARCTIC OCEAN
BERING SEA
BEAUFORT SEA
ALASKA (UNITED STATES)
Yukon Territory
Northwest Territories
British Columbia
Alberta
PACIFIC OCEAN
Washington
Montana
Oregon
Idaho
UNITED STATE
Nevada
Utah
California
Arizona
HAWAII (UNITED STATES)

HABITAT KEY

- Tropical forests
- Deciduous forests
- Coniferous forests
- Tropical grasslands
- Scrublands
- Temperate grasslands
- Desert
- Wetlands
- Tundra
- Ice
- Mangroves

Barrier islands

These long, thin stretches of sand protect the mainland from powerful storms. The barrier islands off the Virginia and Maryland coasts are home to the wild Chincoteague Ponies of Chincoteague and Assateague islands.

Central American rain forest

Rain forests are warm and green all year, and they are home to more than half the world's plants and animals. These colorful scarlet macaws from Costa Rica perch high in rain-forest trees.

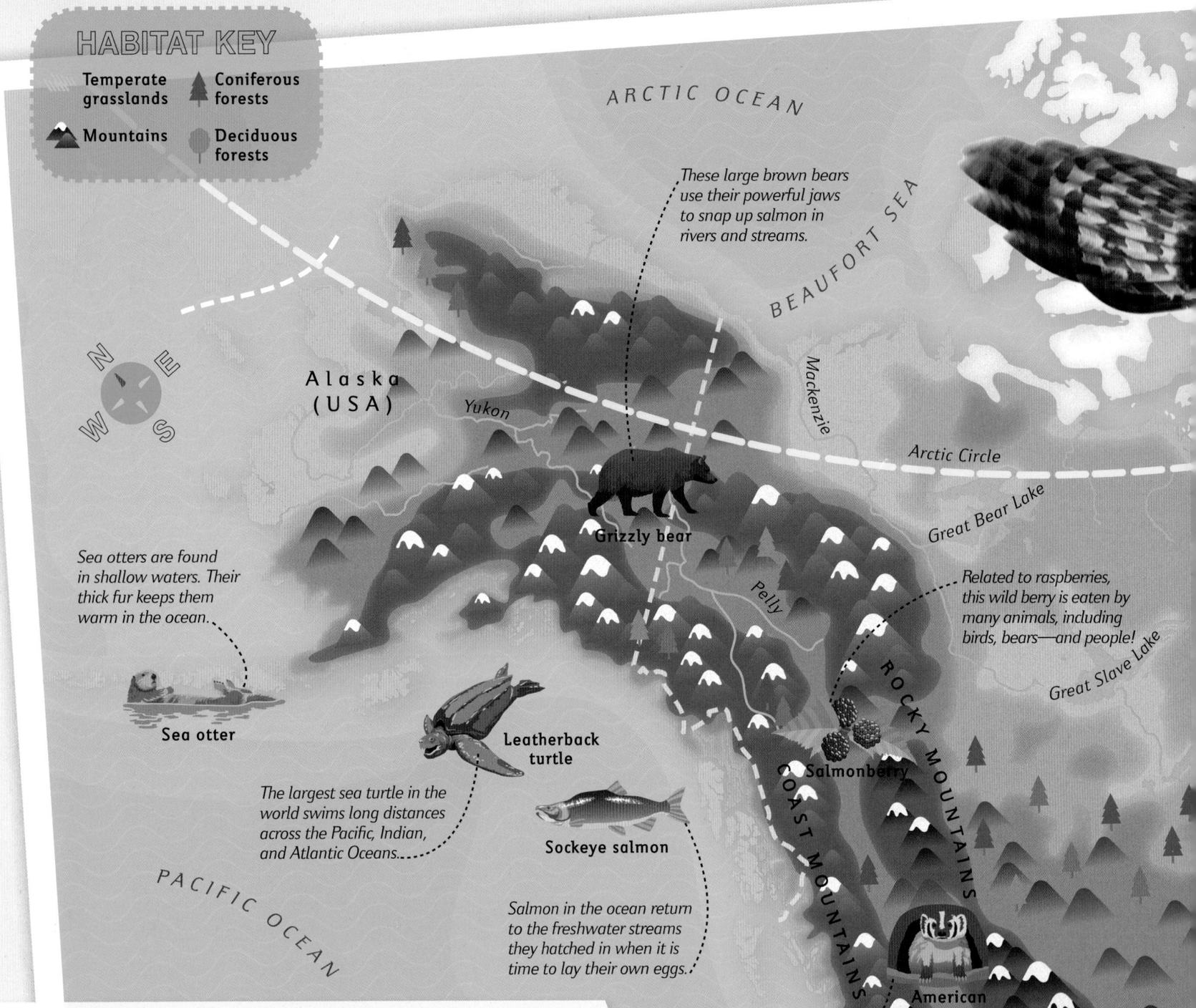

North American taiga

Taiga areas are made of coniferous, or evergreen, forests that grow in some of the northernmost parts of the world. Grizzly bears and gray wolves live in the vast taiga of North America, which stretches across Canada, the world's second-largest country, and Alaska, the largest state in the US.

Location

Most of northern North America is taiga. Summer temperatures reach only 50°F (10°C), and there's lots of snow in the winter.

Great gray owl

North America's tallest owl has a wingspan of up to 5 ft (1.5 m). It listens for rodents moving under the snow, then snatches them up.

Snow geese

Flocks of snow geese turn fields white when they land. These noisy birds live in cold areas, but fly south in large groups during the winter.

Snow geese fly south for the winter.

This flat-tailed mammal fells trees with its teeth. It uses the logs to build dams across rivers, and lodges to live in.

The loon's legs are made for swimming, not walking—so when it wants to fly, it can only take off from water.

A moose can weigh as much as a car! It can also trot at a steady pace of 20 mph (32 kph).

These geese are found all over the world. They have a loud honk and fly in a V-shaped formation.

Both male and female fireflies flash yellow, green, or orange light using special organs in their tails.

Each winter, millions of monarchs migrate from northern North America to Mexico.

Gray wolf

The gray wolf is the largest wild member of the dog family. It can have black, white, tan, brown, or gray fur. It hunts in packs and eats animals from tiny mice to huge moose.

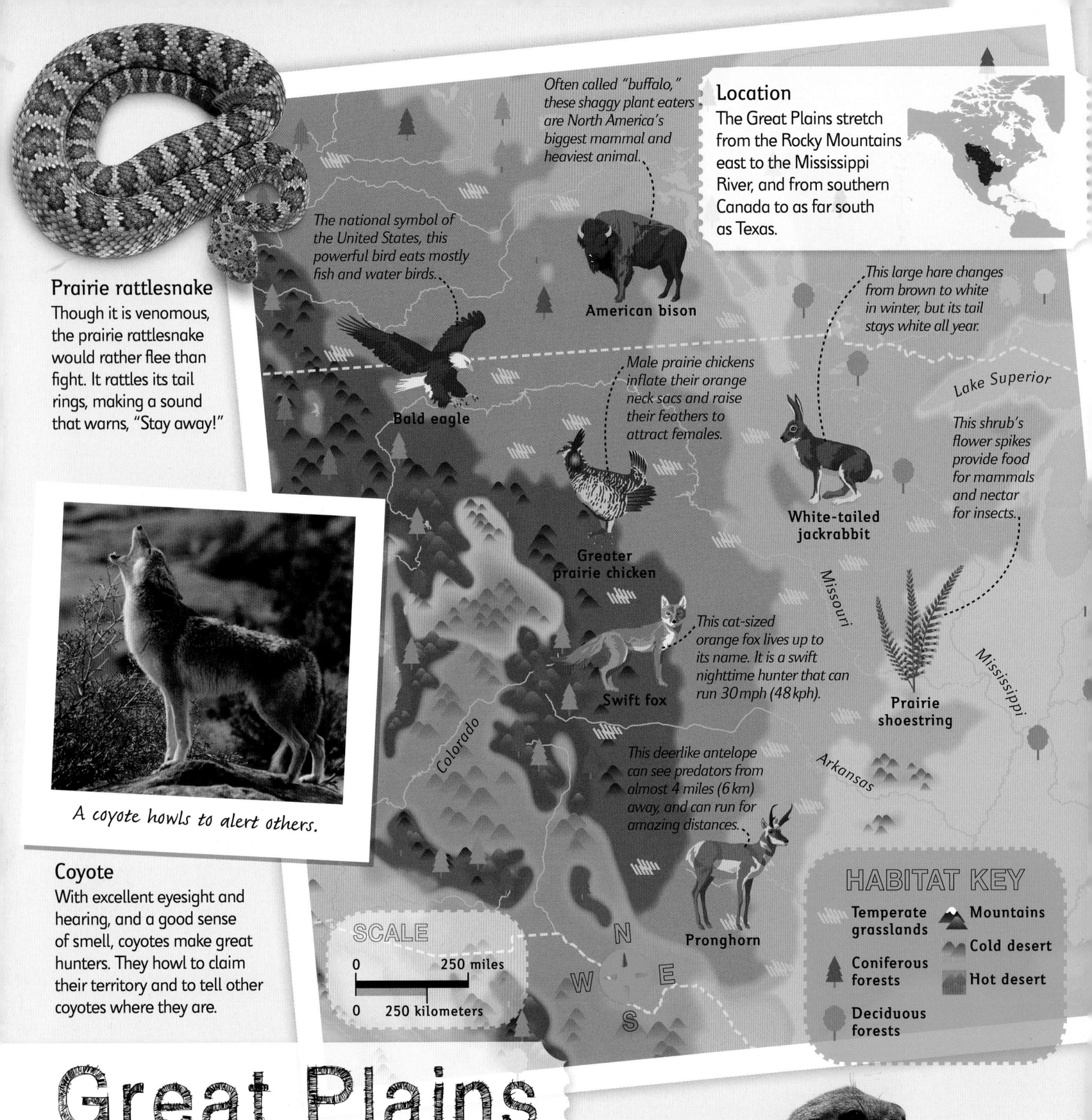

Location

The Great Plains stretch from the Rocky Mountains east to the Mississippi River, and from southern Canada to as far south as Texas.

Prairie rattlesnake

Though it is venomous, the prairie rattlesnake would rather flee than fight. It rattles its tail rings, making a sound that warns, "Stay away!"

A coyote howls to alert others.

Coyote

With excellent eyesight and hearing, and a good sense of smell, coyotes make great hunters. They howl to claim their territory and to tell other coyotes where they are.

Great Plains

The Great Plains are in the center of North America. Made of high prairie about 3,000 miles (4,800 km) long, they were once home to thousands of bison and antelope. Today farmland has taken over much of the area, and mostly cattle herds wander the plains—but wildlife has found ways to survive.

Black-tailed prairie dog

These grass-eating rodents live in underground prairie-dog towns. They greet family with a kiss, and have different warning calls for different predators.

Eastern forests

Deciduous and coniferous forests cover eastern North America. There are mountains and river valleys here, too. Animals have to be smart to survive in areas densely populated with humans.

Gray fox

As big as a medium-sized dog, gray foxes live in broad-leaved forests. They make their dens in hollow trees, and both parents care for the cubs.

If threatened, the skunk sprays a horrible-smelling musk from glands under its tail.

Lake Superior

Sugar maples provide sap for maple syrup. Their leaves turn orange-gold and red in the fall.

Raccoons are highly intelligent. They can live in towns or the country and will eat almost anything!

Lake Michigan

SCALE

0 250 miles

0 250 kilometers

Striped skunk

Only male deer grow antlers. White-tails often escape predators by swimming across lakes or rivers.

Sugar maple

This bright-red bird can sing more than 24 songs. When courting, males offer females the best seeds.

Northern raccoon

Ohio

Northern cardinal

Washington, D.C.

White-tailed deer

This is North America's only marsupial. It can outsmart danger by playing dead for up to four hours.

Mississippi

Virginia opossum

Great horned owl

ATLANTIC OCEAN

This large owl's feathery "horns" look like ears, but its real ears are much farther down on its skull.

HABITAT KEY

- Temperate grasslands
- Coniferous forests
- Tropical grasslands
- Deciduous forests
- Mountains

N W E S

Despite their name, gray squirrels can also have white or reddish fur.

Gray squirrel

Double-jointed ankles help gray squirrels scamper up and down trees. Their teeth never stop growing, so they have to wear them down on nuts and tree bark.

American black bear

Good swimmers and climbers, black bears feast on fruits, nuts, and roots, and sometimes ants and grubs. There are twice as many of them in the world as there are all other bear species combined.

Location

Most of the continent's eastern forests stretch from the Mississippi River Valley eastward, all the way to the Atlantic Ocean.

Western deserts

Western North America has four deserts. These dry, sandy areas are hot during the day, but at night they can get very cold. Animals here must survive these tough conditions—and with very little water.

Turkey vulture

Turkey vultures can't kill their own prey, so they eat animals that have already died instead. Animals that behave in this way are called scavengers.

A turkey vulture perches on a cactus.

Snake

ROCKY MOUNTAINS

USA

Great Salt Lake

SIERRA NEVADA

Colorado

Black-tailed jackrabbit

The jackrabbit can run up to 30 mph (48 kph) and jump 20 ft (6 m) into the air.

Bobcat

A short, or "bobbed," tail gives this wild cat its name. More than a million bobcats live in North America.

Male bighorns fight by crashing their big heads and horns together.

Bighorn sheep

This big, hairy spider lines its desert burrow with silk to keep it from caving in.

Desert blonde tarantula

This lizard lives mostly underground. It has a venomous bite and eats eggs.

Gila monster

Desert broom

The desert broom's flowers provide sweet nectar for butterflies.

A tortoise snacks on a desert plant.

Mohave desert tortoise

This desert tortoise can live for up to 50 years. It digs a burrow to avoid the desert heat, and it spends 95 percent of its time there during the summer.

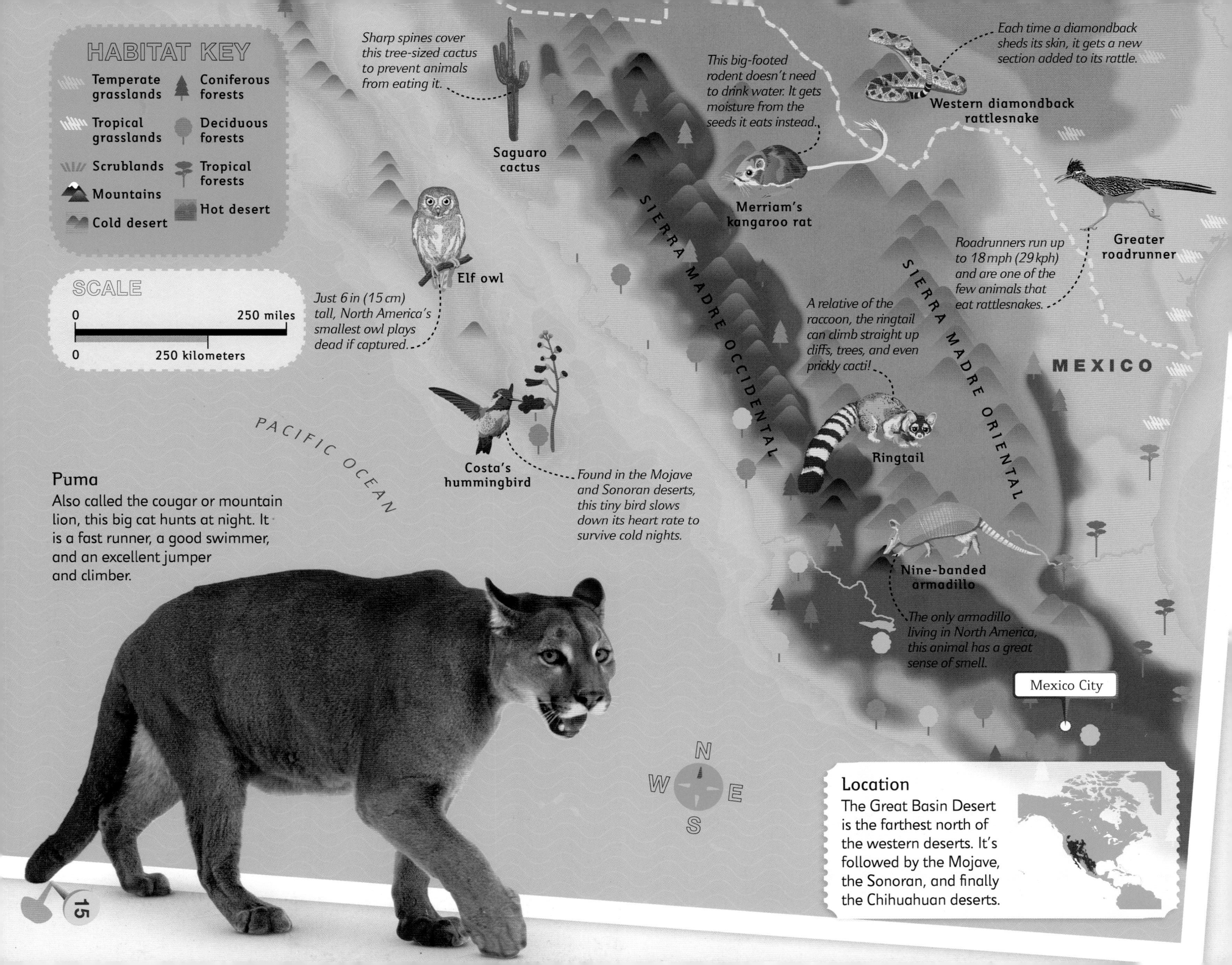
HABITAT KEY
Temperate grasslands
Coniferous forests
Tropical grasslands
Deciduous forests
Scrublands
Tropical forests
Mountains
Hot desert
Cold desert
SCALE
0
250 miles
0
250 kilometers
Sharp spines cover this tree-sized cactus to prevent animals from eating it.
Saguaro cactus
This big-footed rodent doesn't need to drink water. It gets moisture from the seeds it eats instead.
Merriam's kangaroo rat
Each time a diamondback sheds its skin, it gets a new section added to its rattle.
Western diamondback rattlesnake
Elf owl
Just 6 in (15 cm) tall, North America's smallest owl plays dead if captured.
SIERRA MADRE OCCIDENTAL
SIERRA MADRE ORIENTAL
Roadrunners run up to 18 mph (29 kph) and are one of the few animals that eat rattlesnakes.
Greater roadrunner
A relative of the raccoon, the ringtail can climb straight up cliffs, trees, and even prickly cacti!
MEXICO
PACIFIC OCEAN
Costa's hummingbird
Found in the Mojave and Sonoran deserts, this tiny bird slows down its heart rate to survive cold nights.
Ringtail
Nine-banded armadillo
The only armadillo living in North America, this animal has a great sense of smell.
Mexico City
N
W
E
S
Puma
Also called the cougar or mountain lion, this big cat hunts at night. It is a fast runner, a good swimmer, and an excellent jumper and climber.
Location
The Great Basin Desert is the farthest north of the western deserts. It's followed by the Mojave, the Sonoran, and finally the Chihuahuan deserts.

Central America

Seven countries make up the narrow strip of land that is Central America. More than 1,500 different species of birds live here, and many more animals find food and shelter in its warm rain forests.

Ocelot
This fast cat's super sight and hearing help it hunt rabbits and other small animals at night. During the day it rests in the trees, where its markings blend in among the leaves.

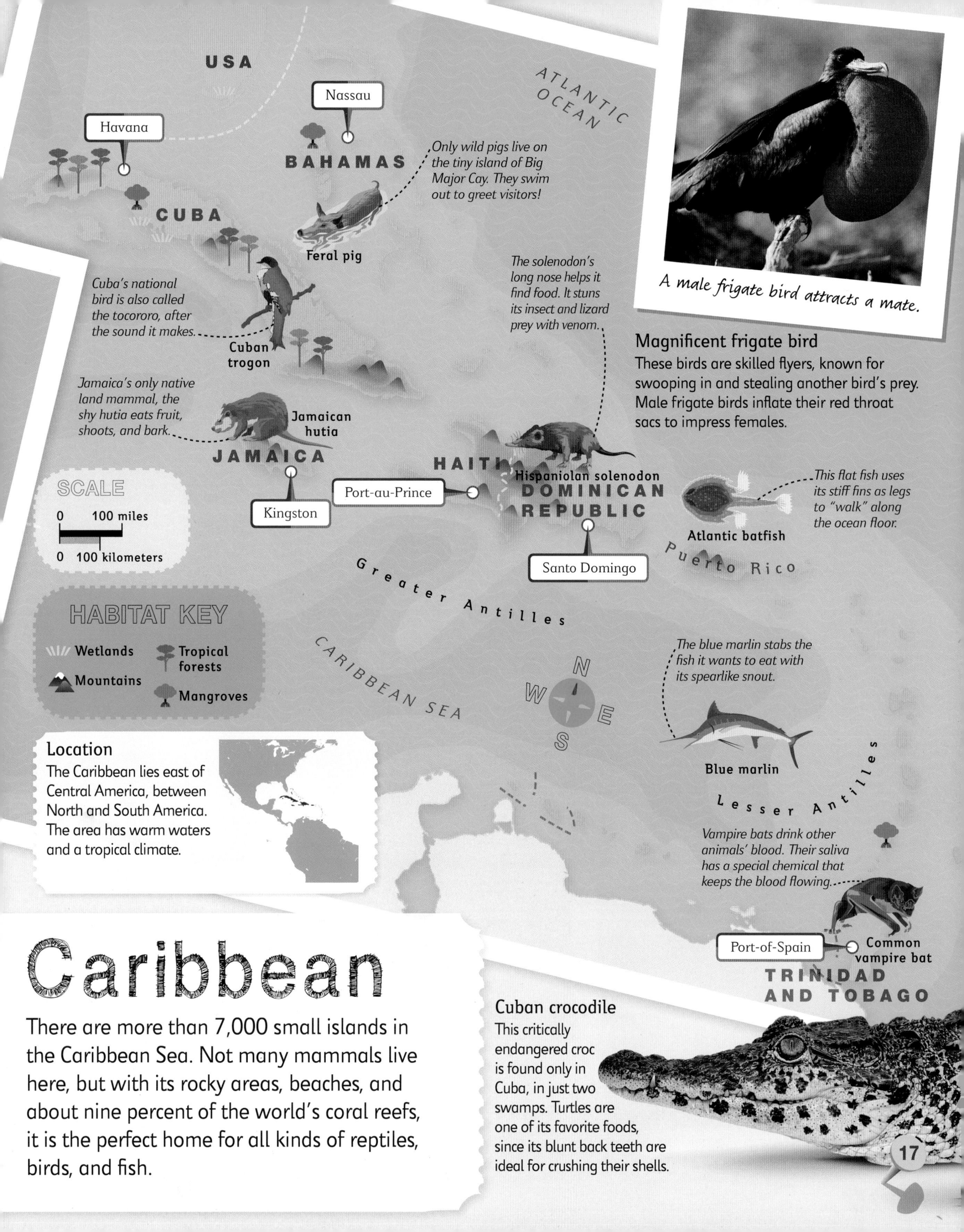

A male frigate bird attracts a mate.

Magnificent frigate bird

These birds are skilled flyers, known for swooping in and stealing another bird's prey. Male frigate birds inflate their red throat sacs to impress females.

Location

The Caribbean lies east of Central America, between North and South America. The area has warm waters and a tropical climate.

Caribbean

There are more than 7,000 small islands in the Caribbean Sea. Not many mammals live here, but with its rocky areas, beaches, and about nine percent of the world's coral reefs, it is the perfect home for all kinds of reptiles, birds, and fish.

Cuban crocodile

This critically endangered croc is found only in Cuba, in just two swamps. Turtles are one of its favorite foods, since its blunt back teeth are ideal for crushing their shells.

Florida Everglades

The Everglades, North America's largest subtropical wetland, is really a big, slow-moving river. The area is half its original size due to humans sending its water to farms and cities. However, it is still home to 350 bird species, and reptiles such as alligators and crocodiles.

Common snapping turtle

Although it has no teeth, this turtle's strong, bony beak and jaws can bite and kill birds, fish, and small mammals. It is also known to bite the heads off other turtles that come too close. No wonder most animals, including humans, know to leave it alone!

Great blue heron North America's largest heron is a slow smover, but it strikes fast to catch fish in mid-swim.

Around 300 fish species are found in the waters of the Everglades, ranging from tiny pygmy sunfish to barracudas that can grow up to 6 ft (2 m) long.

Anhinga This bird hunts underwater. It acts like a spear-fisherman, stabbing fish with its long, sharp bill.

American alligator The Everglades is the only place in the wild where alligators and crocodiles live together.

An alligator's teeth are hidden from sight when its mouth is closed—unlike a crocodile's, which are always visible.

A rat snake shows off its forked tongue.

Everglades rat snake

This long snake both swims and can climb trees. Rats are on its menu, but it also eats frogs, squirrels, and birds and their eggs.

Golden silk orb weaver

Female orb weavers can grow up to 3 in (8 cm) long. Their silk is gold in color, and it is stronger than the material used in bulletproof vests!

Location

The Everglades stretches across the southern tip of Florida. During its rainy season, this area gets twice as much rain as other places in the US.

Green tree frog

Depending on its mood, this little frog is either bright green or dull khaki in color. It inflates its vocal sac and screams if picked up—which can save its life, since the scream makes a lot of predators drop it in surprise!

South America

Earth's fourth-largest continent lies mostly in the southern half of the world. It has tropical rain forests, dry deserts, grassy plains, and high, snowy mountains. The many different habitats means that a variety of amazing animals can make South America their home.

Amazon rain forest

The winding Amazon River flows through the enormous rain forest that shares its name. In addition to producing a fifth of the planet's oxygen, this rain forest is home to an astonishing amount of plants, mammals, birds, and fish.

Pantanal

The Pantanal is a wetland wonderland. With flooded grasslands and tropical forests, it is home to thousands of birds, fish, and reptiles. Mammals also live here, such as the plant-eating capybara, which hides from predators in the muddy waters.

N
W E
S

GALÁPAGOS ISLANDS (ECUADOR)

VENEZUELA
COLOMBIA
ECUADOR
PERU
BOLIVIA
CHILE
ARGENTINA
PACIFIC OCEAN

HABITAT KEY

- Tropical forests
- Deciduous forests
- Tropical grasslands
- Scrublands
- Temperate grasslands
- Deserts
- Wetlands
- Mountains
- Mangroves

Patagonian steppe

Shared between Argentina and southern Chile, the warm, dry Patagonian steppe is filled with shrubs as well as grasses. It makes a good home for mammals, ranging from tiny rodents to foxes and mountain lions.

Pampas

Its acres of grassland mean the pampas attracts a lot of wildlife, particularly birds. Some, like the flightless Darwin's rhea, graze on plants. It also eats frogs and insects that might be hiding in the grass.

Andes

Although parts are warm with plenty of plants, the Andean mountains are mostly full of high, rugged places. Animals need to be tough and adaptable to live here. Flamingos, for example, can manage to find food in even the saltiest lakes.

Amazon rain forest

The Amazon is the Earth's largest tropical rain forest, and it surrounds one of the world's largest rivers—the Amazon River. Lots of species live here, including more than 430 mammals, 1,300 birds, 3,000 fish, 870 reptiles and amphibians, and 2.5 million insects!

A young collared anteater rides on its mother's back.

Collared anteater

This tree-climbing anteater doesn't have any teeth. Instead it slurps up ants and termites with a tongue that can be 16 in (40 cm) long!

Yellow-banded poison dart frog

This frog's bright-yellow color tells predators to keep away. It is a serious warning, since its skin gives off toxic chemicals that can kill other animals.

Caracas

VENEZUELA

Orinoco

GUIANA HIGHLANDS

Bogotá

COLOMBIA

One of the largest beetles in the world, the Hercules can get up to 7 in (18 cm) long.

Hercules beetle

Quito

ECUADOR

This tree can grow 13 ft (4 m) a year. It is pollinated by rain-forest bats.

Also called botos, these rare dolphins hunt catfish in the Amazon and Orinoco Rivers.

Kapok tree

Pink river dolphin

PERU

Just 9–10 in (23–26 cm) long, this little primate eats mostly fruit, insects, and plants.

This giant blue butterfly has a wingspan of 5–8 in (13–20 cm).

ANDES

PACIFIC OCEAN

Emperor tamarin

Blue morpho

Lima

La Paz

Sucre

HABITAT KEY

- Wetlands
- Tropical grasslands
- Mountains
- Tropical forests
- Deciduous forests
- Mangroves

N W E S

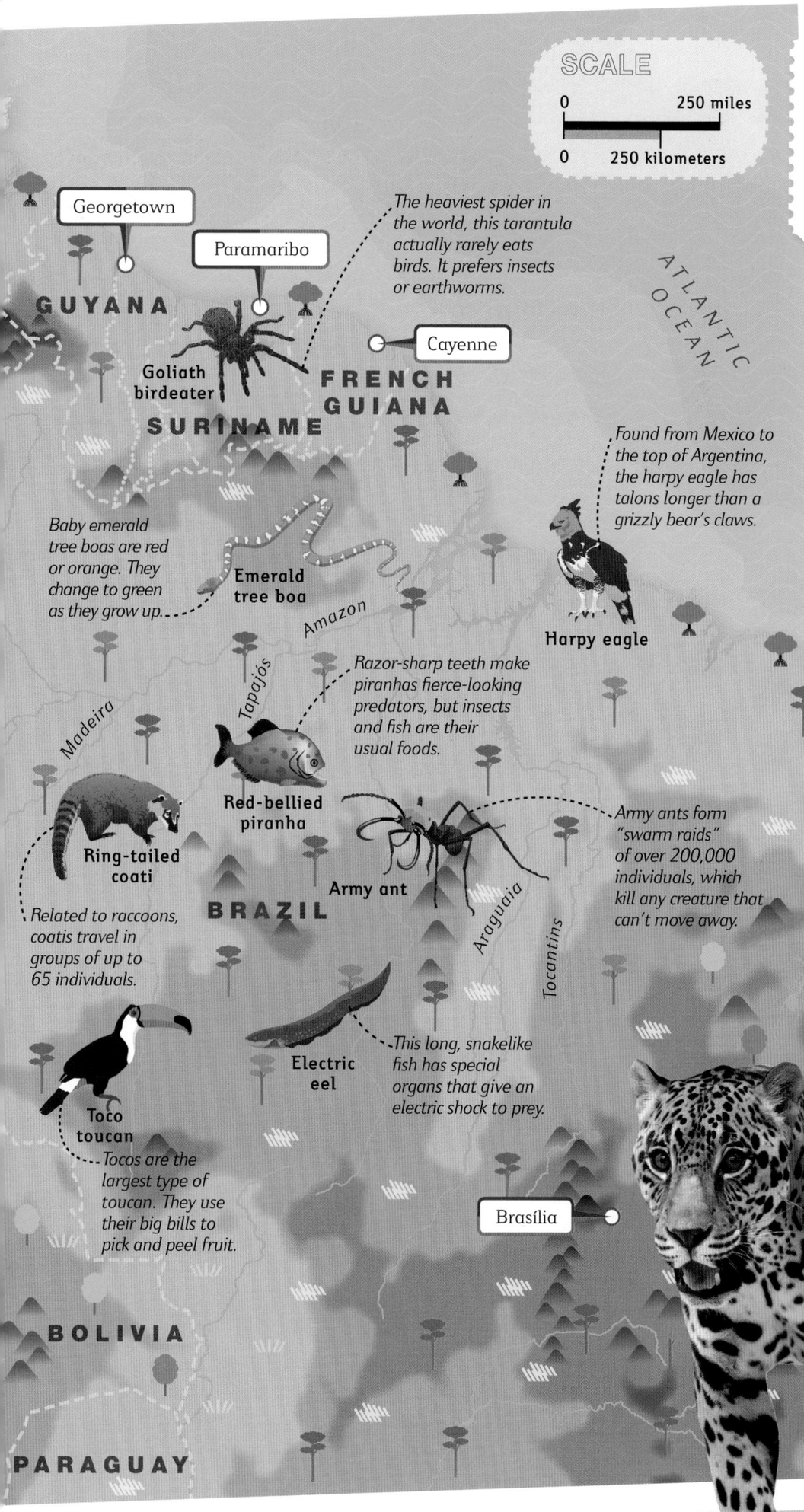

Location

Most of the Amazon is found in Brazil, but it extends into eight other countries. It is very hot and wet—it rains more than 200 days a year here.

The red howler monkey eats leaves and fruit.

Red howler monkey

Red howlers live up to their name. They are the loudest animals on land, and their howls can be heard 3 miles (5 km) away!

Jaguar

Jaguars are so good at hiding that scientists don't know how many exist in the wild. They are found throughout Central America and the northern half of South America.

Andean mountains

The Andes is one of the highest mountain ranges in the world. It reaches a top height of 22,831 ft (6,959 m) and stretches along the west coast of South America. Animals here have to cope with extreme habitats, from glaciers to tropical forests.

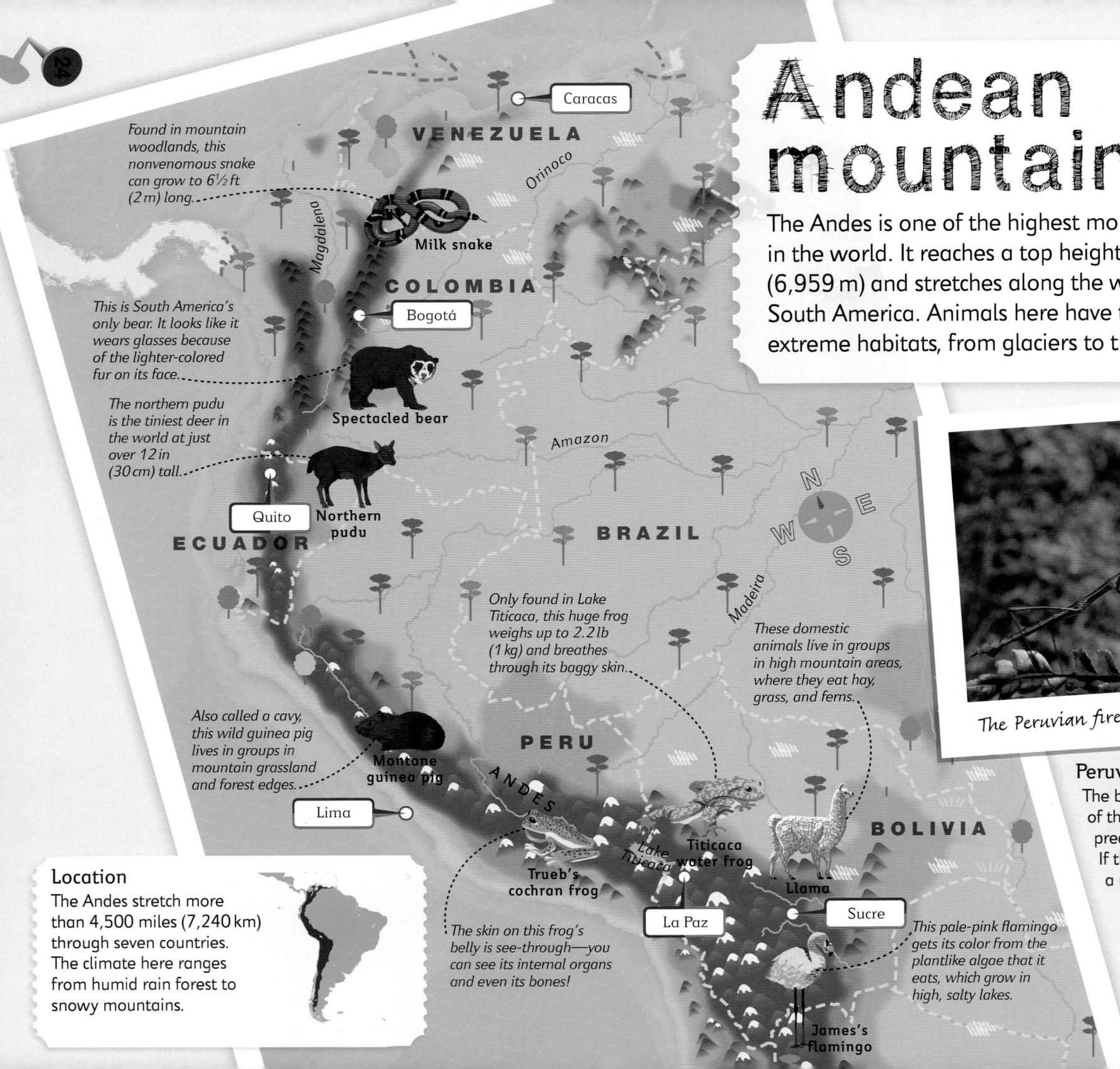

The Peruvian firestick eats ferns.

Peruvian firestick

The bright-red color of this stick insect warns predators to stay away. If threatened, it releases a nasty-smelling liquid.

Location

The Andes stretch more than 4,500 miles (7,240 km) through seven countries. The climate here ranges from humid rain forest to snowy mountains.

The male cock of the rock can extend the crest on its head.

Andean cock of the rock

Male cock of the rocks are brilliant orange, while females are brownish. The males gather together to show off their feathers to females, who pick their favorite from the group.

Vicuña

These small members of the camel family are so well-adapted to their mountain homes that they can survive at altitudes as high as 16,404 ft (5,000 m).

HABITAT KEY

- Wetlands
- Scrublands
- Temperate grasslands
- Tropical grasslands
- Deciduous forests
- Mountains
- Cold desert

ARGENTINA

Mountain caracara

Caracaras often wander around, turning over stones to look for insects, rodents, and other animals to eat.

Santiago

This goose's blood absorbs more oxygen than other geese, so it can survive at high altitudes where there is less oxygen in the air.

Andean goose

Colorado

Negro

Chubut

PACIFIC OCEAN

CHILE

ANDES

The Andean condor is the world's largest flying bird. It rides mountain air currents with a wingspan of up to 10½ ft (3.2 m).

Andean condor

SOUTH ATLANTIC OCEAN

Short legs allow this endangered deer to clamber over rough, high mountain terrain. It is the national animal of Chile.

Huemul

Also known as the zorro, these foxlike wild dogs hunt lizards, insects, rabbits, and geese. They make their dens in rocky caves.

Culpeo

Falkland Islands

SCALE

0 250 miles

0 250 kilometers

Long-tailed chinchilla

With 60 hairs growing out of each follicle, this rodent has very thick fur. Having thick fur is ideal for the cold temperatures of the high Andes.

Temperate pampas

With level plains as far as the eye can see, it's no wonder native South Americans named this region pampas—meaning "flat surface." This temperate grassland provides plenty of seeds for birds, insects, and small mammals to eat.

Eyes high on its head allow the coypu to see when it swims.

Coypu

Sometimes mistaken for a beaver, the coypu is a water-loving rodent that can get up to 3 ft (1 m) long. Also called the "nutria," it lives in riverside burrows and eats plants.

Argentine horned frog

At 5½ in (14 cm) long and weighing up to 1 lb (480 g), the horned frog is big enough to eat lizards, mice, and even other horned frogs.

This lizard gets up to 4½ ft (1.4 m) long. During the day it hunts for snails, spiders, and insects.

Argentine black and white teju

SIERRAS DE CÓRDOBA

This bloodsucking bug feeds on rodents, marsupials, and even humans. It sometimes passes on a parasite that causes disease.

Assassin bug

Mollina's hog-nosed skunk

This skunk uses its broad, fleshy nose to snuffle out beetles and spiders to eat.

Desaguadero

This medium-sized fox throws itself to the ground and plays dead if danger passes.

Pampas fox

ARGENTINA

With yellow, white, green, blue, red, and black feathers, this is one of the most colorful birds to live in the reedbeds of the pampas.

Many-colored rush-tyrant

The greater rhea can reach 4½ ft (1.4 m) tall. It can't fly, but it can run as fast as 37 mph (60 kph).

Greater rhea

The long, powerful legs of this large rodent allow it to run up to 30 mph (48 kph).

Patagonian mara

Colorado

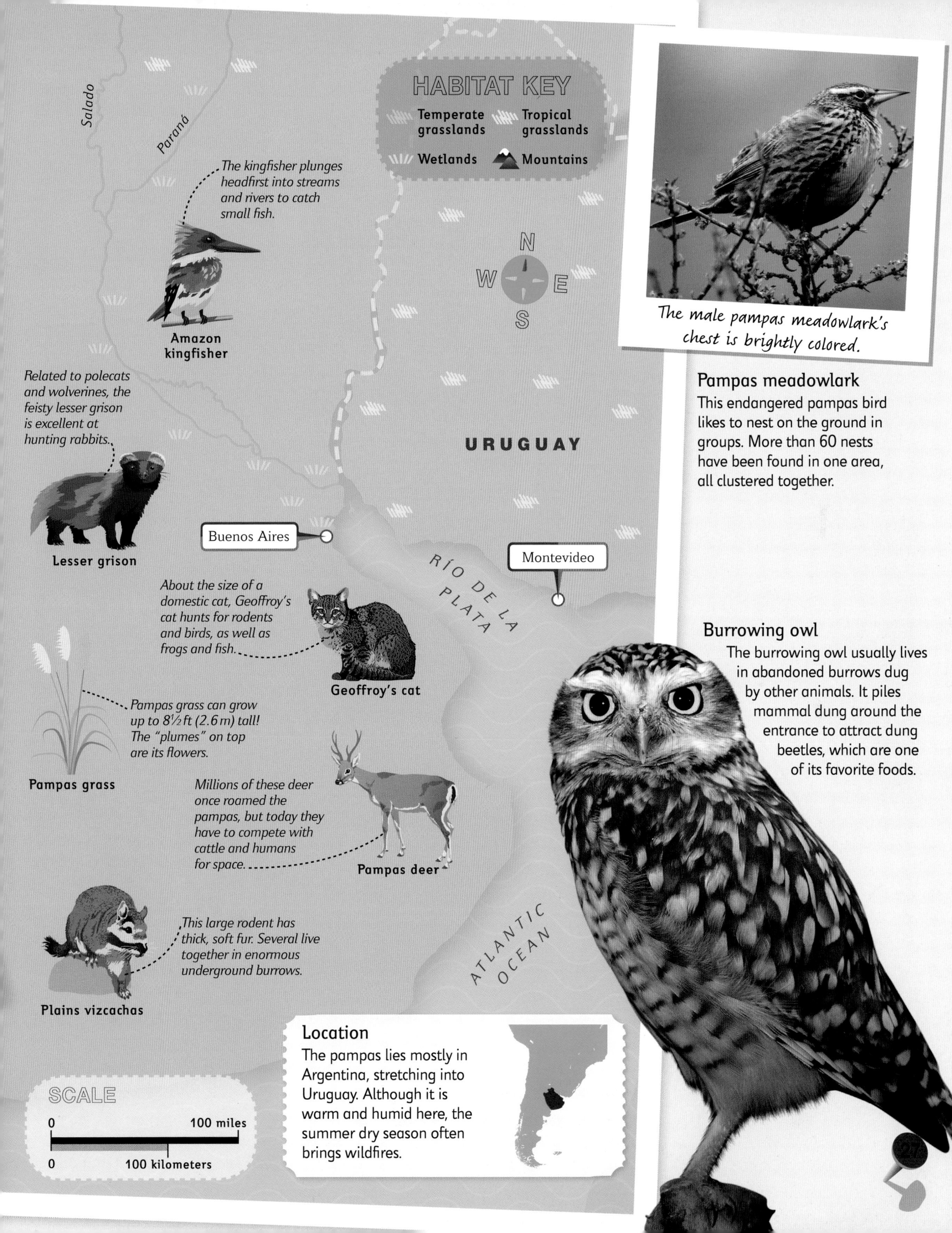

The male pampas meadowlark's chest is brightly colored.

Pampas meadowlark

This endangered pampas bird likes to nest on the ground in groups. More than 60 nests have been found in one area, all clustered together.

Burrowing owl

The burrowing owl usually lives in abandoned burrows dug by other animals. It piles mammal dung around the entrance to attract dung beetles, which are one of its favorite foods.

Location

The pampas lies mostly in Argentina, stretching into Uruguay. Although it is warm and humid here, the summer dry season often brings wildfires.

Pantanal

The Pantanal is the world's largest wetland, which means a lot of it is underwater for much of the year. The 3,500 different plant species that grow here make it an ideal home for lots of birds and mammals, including the capybara, which is a giant relative of the guinea pig.

Jabiru stork

The jabiru is the tallest flying bird in South and Central America, and can grow to over 3 ft (1 m) high. It grabs fish, frogs, and insects with its enormous bill.

A jabiru stork wades through the Pantanal.

N
W E
S

HABITAT KEY

- Tropical grasslands
- Deciduous forests
- Wetlands

This big freshwater snail grows up to 6 in (15 cm) long! It only comes out of the water at night to find food.

Channeled apple snail

About as big as a medium-sized dog, the capybara is the world's largest rodent.

Capybara

Paraguay

The roseate spoonbill sweeps its spoon-shaped bill from side to side to scoop up minnows—tiny freshwater fish.

Anacondas live in and out of water. They can be up to 29½ ft (9 m) long, but hide among water plants to surprise prey.

Green anaconda

BOLIVIA

BRAZIL

Roseate spoonbill

The marsh deer has broad hooves that spread out to prevent them from sinking in marshy ground.

Marsh deer

SCALE

0 — 50 miles

0 — 50 kilometers

This wetland plant's leaves can grow to 8 ft (2.5 m) across, and can hold an animal weighing up to 45 lb (20.5 kg)!

Giant water lily

This clever monkey uses rocks to crack nuts and crush crab shells to get at the food inside.

Hooded capuchin

Location

The Pantanal lies south of the Amazon rain forest in Brazil, Bolivia, and Paraguay. It gets so much rain that 80 percent of it is flooded during the rainy season.

PARAGUAY

Giant otter

Found only in South American rivers and rain forests, giant otters get up to 4½ ft (1.4 m) long. They eat fish, crabs, and even small caimans!

Yacare caiman

Caiman look like their alligator relatives, but have a pointier snout. The yacare gets up to 10 ft (3 m) long. Its favorite food is the piranha, but it also eats apple snails.

Galápagos

The Galápagos are a group of volcanic islands that lie about 621 miles (1,000 km) off the coast of Ecuador. There are several larger islands and many more smaller ones. Three major ocean currents meet here, bringing in lots of different sea animals.

Darwin Island

Wolf Island

Location

The Galápagos islands cluster around the equator in the Pacific Ocean. They have two seasons—a cool, dry season and a warm season.

PACIFIC OCEAN

Marchena Island

More lava lizards live in the Galápagos than any other reptile. They warm themselves on sunny rocks.

Galápagos lava lizard

Although it can't fly, this cormorant is a powerful swimmer and hunts eels and octopuses on the ocean floor.

Flightless cormorant

Bright-blue feet make this bird easy to spot. Female boobies have darker-blue feet than males.

Blue-footed booby

San Salvador Island

Fernandina Island

Galápagos hawk

The Galápagos hawk is very rare. It mostly eats giant centipedes, but also catches rodents and young iguanas.

Santa Cruz Island

Galápagos sea lion

This sea lion can move its back flippers independently, so it can "gallop" on land.

This little penguin lives farther north than any other penguin species.

Galápagos penguin

Isabela Island

San Cristóbal Island

Galápagos tortoise

This tortoise can grow up to 5 ft (1.5 m) long and weigh up to 500 lb (227 kg). Some of them are over 100 years old!

Santa María Island

Española Island

A marine iguana grazes on seaweed.

Marine iguana

Marine iguanas are the only lizards to swim in the ocean, where they look for seaweed to eat. Special glands clean salt from their blood, which they sneeze out!

Sally Lightfoot crab

This bright-red crab earned its name by scuttling around at high speeds. It hides from birds by squeezing into tiny spaces between rocks.

N W E S

SCALE

0 25 miles

0 25 kilometers

Cerrado

The Cerrado is found almost entirely in Brazil. It is made up of mostly tropical grassland, but a few trees are mixed with it in places, and there are areas of dry forest, too. With more than 10,000 different plant species, the Cerrado offers plenty of food and shelter for lots of animals.

Both male and female hyacinth macaws are bright blue.

Hyacinth macaw

The longest parrot on the planet, the hyacinth macaw can be 3 ft (1 m) long. Their large bills are able to crack even the hardest palm nuts.

Leaf-cutting ants

These ants "saw" leaves into pieces with their jaws. They carry the bits back to their underground home, where a fungus grows on them, which the ants harvest and eat.

HABITAT KEY

- Wetlands
- Tropical forests
- Tropical grasslands
- Deciduous forests
- Mountains
- Cold desert

N W E S

BRAZIL

Tapajós

BOLIVIA

PARAGUAY

Often called "a fox on stilts," the maned wolf's long legs help it to see over the tall Cerrado grass.

Maned wolf

The giant anteater uses its sticky tongue to lap up 35,000 ants and termites a day!

Giant anteater

King vultures don't have a great sense of smell. To make up for it, they follow other vultures to lead them to dead animals to eat.

King vulture

Boettger's caecilian

Although it has no legs, this isn't a snake, but an amphibian that lives underground.

Only the male helmeted manakin has this flashy red crest. The female is a plain gray-green bird.

Helmeted manakin

Found all over Central America and the north of South America, this lizard spends most of its life in trees, where it eats tender green leaves.

Green iguana

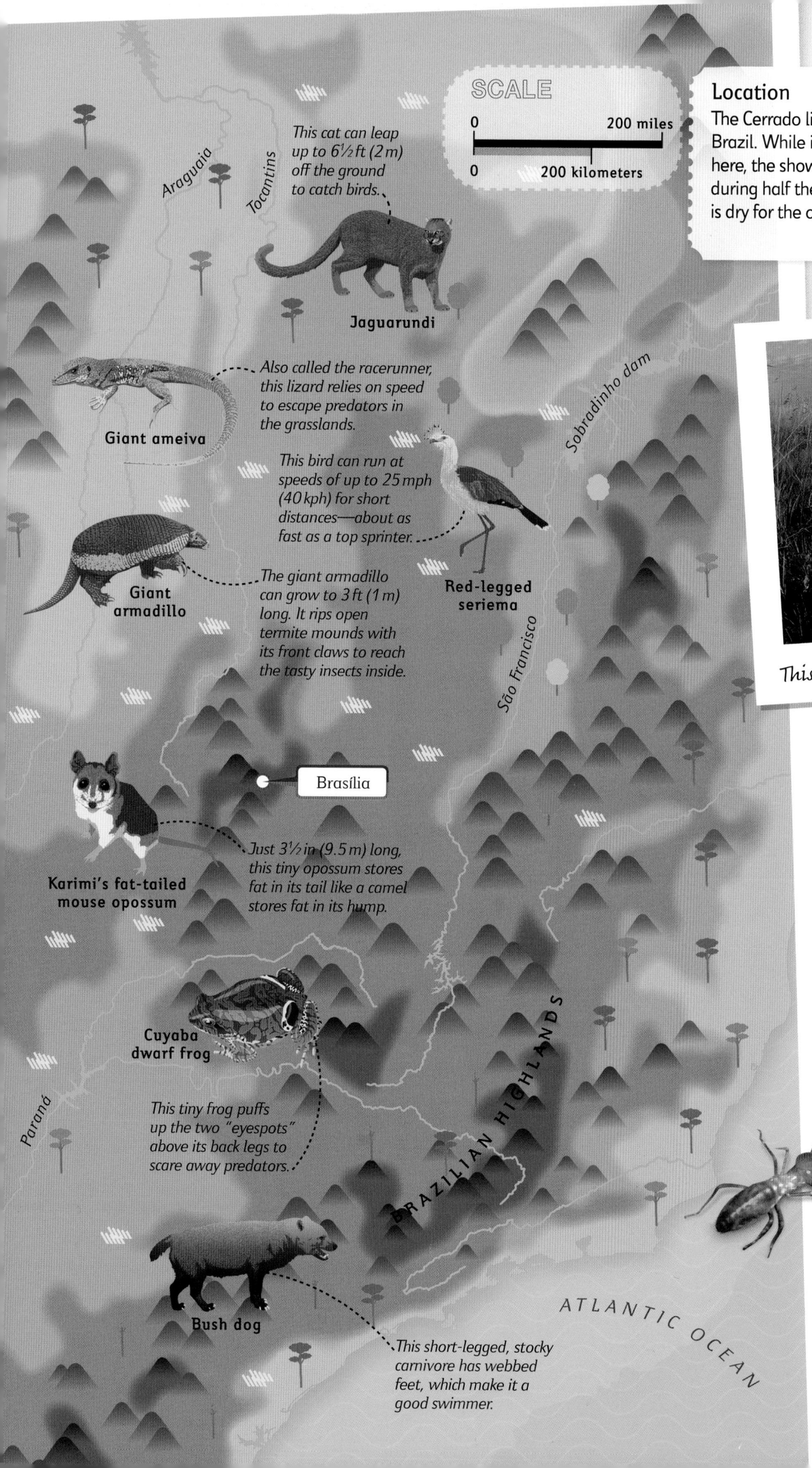

Location

The Cerrado lies in central Brazil. While it rains a lot here, the showers only fall during half the year, so it is dry for the other half.

This mound houses a termite colony.

Termites

Termites are ant-sized insects that build their own "cities." These huge mounds get up to 30 in (77 cm) high. The mounds have underground chambers where workers store wood, care for eggs, and even grow fungal gardens for food!

Cordillera Blanca

Part of the Andes, this is the largest tropical mountain range in the world. Peaks over 19,685 ft (6,000 m) high surround valleys filled with lakes and streams. There isn't much oxygen at these heights, so it is hard to breathe, but the animals here manage surprisingly well.

Andean condor Female condors produce just one egg every two years. It takes almost 60 days for the egg to hatch.

Taruca

You can tell a taruca apart from other deer by the dark, Y-shaped mark on its face. It feeds on mountain grasses, and travels into valleys to find water.

Guanaco The guanaco is a member of the camel family. Movable pads on its hooves help it walk over rocky ground.

The guanaco is the ancestor of domestic llamas. The closely related vicuña is the ancestor of domestic alpacas.

Andean goose The Andean goose lives in mountain wetlands, but it doesn't swim well, so it avoids the water!

Colocolo The colocolo is a nocturnal predator that hunts rodents, guinea pigs, and ground-nesting birds.

Vizcachas are related to chinchillas.

Southern mountain vizcacha

The rabbitlike vizcacha spends a lot of time on rocky ledges, basking in the sun. It is covered in thick, soft fur all the way to the end of its curled tail.

The colocolo resembles a house cat, but can be identified by the dark-colored bands and lines around its legs.

Mountain caracara This black-and-white bird of prey builds nests of sticks on cliff ledges in the high Andes.

Torrent duck

Native to the Andes, the torrent duck plunges in and out of cold, fast-moving mountain streams to catch insect larvae to eat. Females, like this one, are orange, but males are black and white.

The spectacled bear lives only in the Andean mountains.

Spectacled bear The spectacled bear eats fruit, flowers, and plants. It also hunts insects, rodents, and birds in grassland habitats.

Culpeo The culpeo spends most of its time alone, but parents stay together to raise cubs in mountain dens.

Location

The Cordillera Blanca is a chain of mountains in northern Peru. Snow covers many of them, and temperatures range from 37–73°F (3–23°C).

Giant hummingbirds are the biggest hummingbirds in the world.

Giant hummingbird

Giant hummingbirds get up to 8½ in (21.5 cm) long! They mostly feed on nectar from flowers, looking for the ones with the highest levels of energy-filled sugar. They also eat spiders and small insects.

Africa

This continent is so large and has so many different habitats, it feels as if there are several Africas, not just one. With deserts and rain forests, mountains and grasslands, Africa is home to some of the best-known—and most endangered—species on Earth.

African savanna
Africa's tropical grassland is known as savanna. It is often what people think of when they imagine Africa: vast, open, grassy plains. Lots of hoofed animals live here, moving around in search of fresh grass—or, in the giraffe's case, tender acacia leaves to eat.

South African fynbos
The southwest tip of South Africa is covered with shrubs and heathland known as fynbos. Animals such as tortoises, frogs, and small baboons live among the 9,000 plant species that grow here. That's more plant species than in South America's Amazon rain forest!

Canary Islands (SPAIN)
MOROCCO
TUNISIA
ALGERIA
WESTERN SAHARA
MAURITANIA
MALI
NIGER
CAPE VERDE
SENEGAL
THE GAMBIA
GUINEA-BISSAU
GUINEA
BURKINA FASO
ATLANTIC OCEAN
SIERRA LEONE
LIBERIA
IVORY COAST
GHANA
TOGO
BENIN
NIGERIA
CAMEROON
GULF OF GUINEA
Bioco
EQUATORIAL GUINEA
São Tomé & Príncipe
GABON
CONGO

N
W E
S

HABITAT KEY
- Tropical forests
- Deciduous forests
- Coniferous forests
- Tropical grasslands
- Scrublands
- Deserts
- Wetlands
- Mountains
- Mangroves

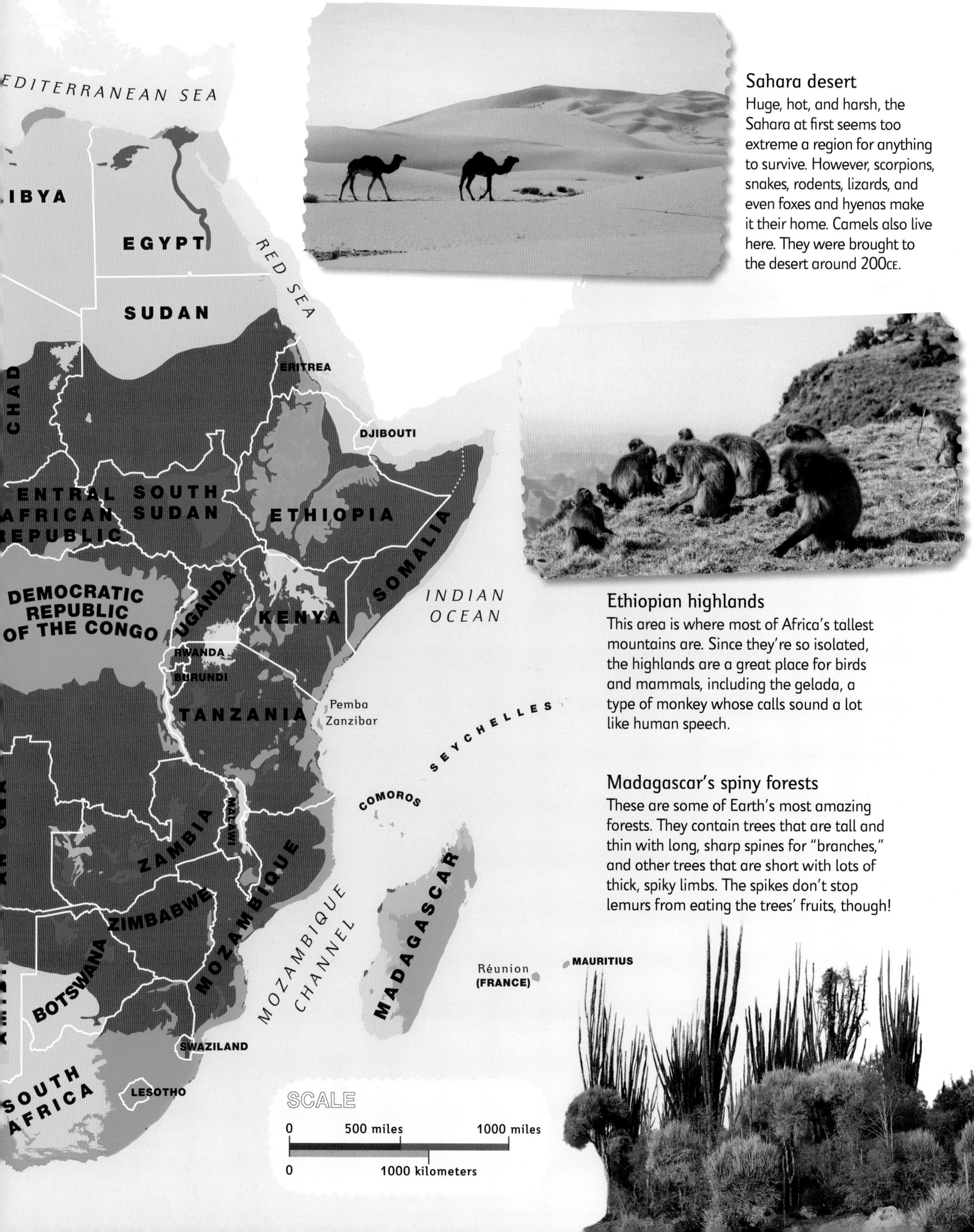

Sahara desert

Huge, hot, and harsh, the Sahara at first seems too extreme a region for anything to survive. However, scorpions, snakes, rodents, lizards, and even foxes and hyenas make it their home. Camels also live here. They were brought to the desert around 200CE.

Ethiopian highlands

This area is where most of Africa's tallest mountains are. Since they're so isolated, the highlands are a great place for birds and mammals, including the gelada, a type of monkey whose calls sound a lot like human speech.

Madagascar's spiny forests

These are some of Earth's most amazing forests. They contain trees that are tall and thin with long, sharp spines for "branches," and other trees that are short with lots of thick, spiky limbs. The spikes don't stop lemurs from eating the trees' fruits, though!

Sahara desert

The Sahara is the Earth's largest hot desert. It covers 3,630,000 sq miles (9,400,000 sq km) and is home to about 70 animal and 500 plant species. They have to deal with temperatures as high as 135°F (57°C) and very little rainfall.

Fennec fox
This small fox's huge ears aren't only great for hearing. They also help to keep the fox cool by releasing its body heat into the air.

HABITAT KEY
Tropical grasslands
Wetlands
Scrublands
Mountains
Hot desert

Tunis
N
W
E
S
MEDITERRANEAN SEA
IA
Tripoli
This scorpion's venom is highly toxic, but it is rarely fatal to humans.
Deathstalker scorpion
LIBYA
Cairo
EGYPT
This crocodile gets up to 20 ft (6 m) long, weighs 2,205 lb (1,000 kg), and lives up to 40 years.
Nile crocodile
Nile
RED SEA
The tiny hopping jerboa's hind legs are four times longer than its front ones.
Lesser Egyptian jerboa
AÏR MOUNTAINS
TIBESTI MOUNTAINS
Found in southern desert shrubland, the Nubian bustard eats large insects, leaves, fruit, and grass seeds.
The Dorcas gazelle never has to drink. It gets all its moisture from eating flowers, leaves, and bark.
Dorcas gazelle
Sandy-colored markings make it easy for this bird to hide from desert predators.
The largest tortoise in Africa, this reptile can weigh up to 231 lbs (105 kg).
African spurred tortoise
Chestnut-bellied sandgrouse
ERITREA
Khartoum
Asmara
Nubian bustard
CHAD
SUDAN
ETHIOPIA
NIGERIA
N'Djamena
Chari

Location

The Sahara stretches across North Africa, from the Atlantic Ocean in the west all the way to the Red Sea in the east.

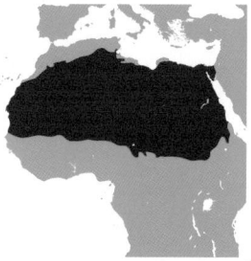

Dromedary camel

Dromedaries are well suited to the desert. They can store fat in their hump as food, have thick eyelashes to keep sand out of their eyes, and can drink 40 gallons (182 liters) of water without stopping!

Dromedary camels have only one hump.

Congo Basin

Often called "Africa's Green Heart," the Congo Basin is a huge area of land surrounding the Congo River. This supports the world's second-largest rain forest, and, along with swamps and lakes, it is a haven for hundreds of amazing animals—including bonobos and chimpanzees, the closest living relatives of humans.

Emperor scorpion
At 8 in (20 cm) long, the emperor is the largest scorpion on the planet. Surprisingly, despite its big size, its sting is not deadly for humans.

CHAD

SOUTH SUDAN

CENTRAL AFRICAN REPUBLIC

CAMEROON

GABON

CONGO

DEMOCRATIC REPUBLIC OF THE CONGO

UGANDA

RWANDA

MBANG MOUNTAINS

ADAMAWA HIGHLANDS

Ubangi

Congo

Lake Albert

Lake Edward

Bangui

Yaoundé

Juba

Kigali

HABITAT KEY

- Wetlands
- Mangroves
- Tropical grasslands
- Tropical forests
- Mountains

Violet turaco
The turaco gets its bright colors from copper, a metal found in the plants that it eats.

Leopard
This big cat stashes its prey up trees to keep it out of reach of other predators.

African buffalo
If one buffalo is attacked by a lion, the rest of its herd will rush to defend it.

Bongo
Timid bongos have many stripes that look like light and shade, so they can hide easily in dense rain forests.

Okapi
Although its legs are striped like a zebra's, the secretive okapi is a close relative of the giraffe.

Western gorilla
Adult male gorillas are called "silverbacks" because of the silvery-white hair that covers their backs.

Mandrill
The mandrill has the most colorful face in the monkey world—and a bluish-purple bottom!

Bonobo
This slender, peaceful ape eats less meat than its chimpanzee cousins and spends more time in trees.

African grey parrot
One of the world's most intelligent birds, gentle African greys can learn lots of human words.

Brazzaville

Kinshasa

Kasai

ATLANTIC OCEAN

Luanda

N
W E
S

Slender lungfish

The lungfish lives in floodplains that often dry up. During these times, it uses its lungs to breathe air until the water returns.

This tiny bloodsucker causes more deaths than any other creature because it passes on the disease malaria.

Anopheles mosquito

ANGOLA

Covered in protective scales, the pangolin rolls itself into a ball when threatened.

Common pangolin

This eagle swoops down on fish from nearby trees, grabbing them in its sharp talons.

African fish eagle

Congo

BURUNDI

TANZANIA

MITUMBA MOUNTAINS

Lake Tanganyika

ZAMBIA

SCALE

0 200 miles

0 200 kilometers

Location

The Congo Basin is located around the equator in west-central Africa. There are hot, humid places, and cooler, dry ones. Some parts also get a lot of rain.

White-throated bee-eater

The bee-eater lives in large families. It rubs bees and wasps against a hard surface to remove their stings before eating them.

Chimpanzees are one of the closest living relatives of humans.

Chimpanzee

This smart ape lives in family groups and can walk on two legs as well as four. It uses tools, such as rocks and sticks, to help it get food.

Red river hog

Red river hogs move around mostly at night, returning to burrows during the day to keep cool. They live in noisy family groups called sounders.

The red river hog uses its snout to sniff out tasty roots in the ground.

Southern savanna

Much of southern Africa is covered in tropical grasslands called savanna. They're great places to find grazing animals, such as zebras and antelopes. This also means that they attract predators, such as lions.

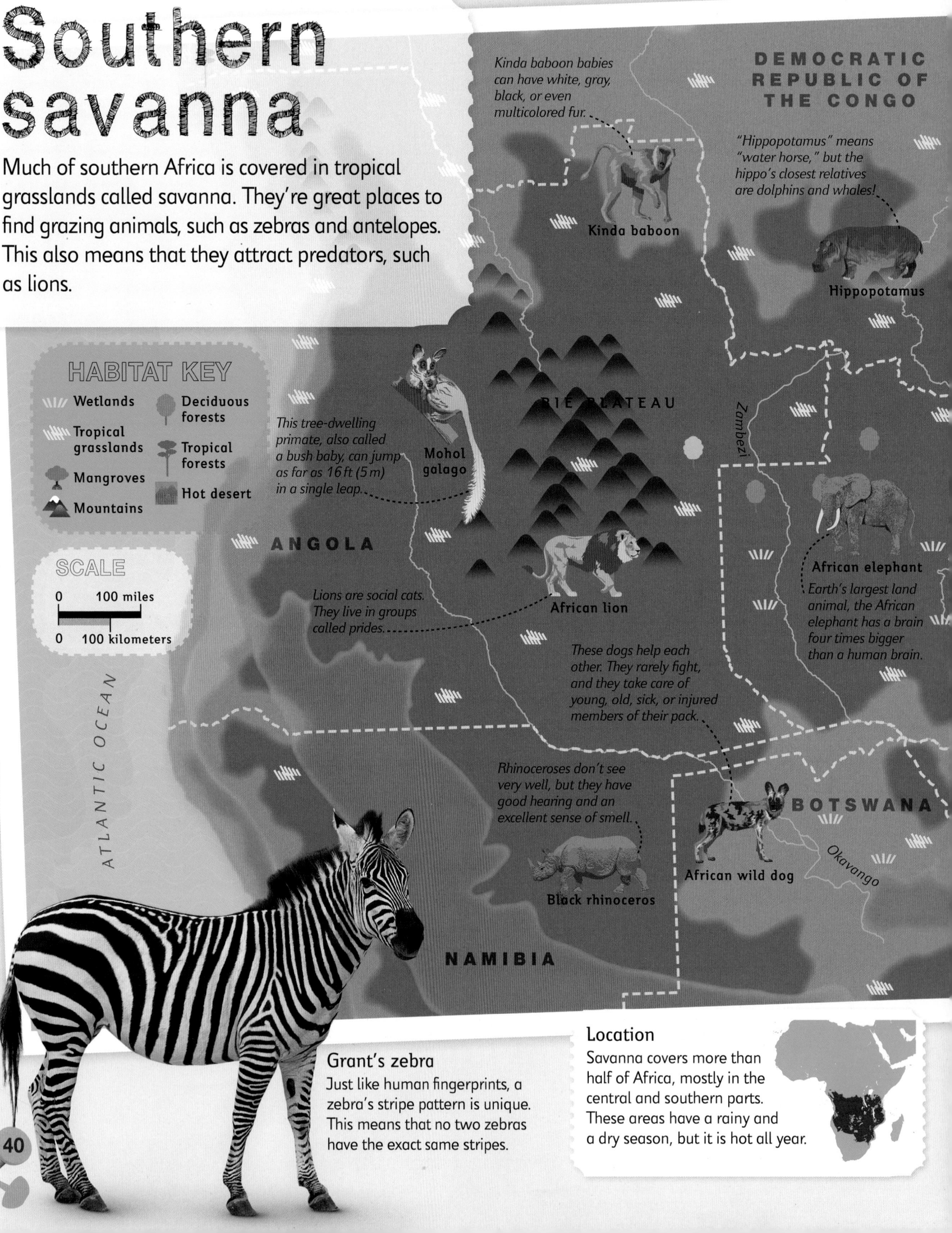

Grant's zebra

Just like human fingerprints, a zebra's stripe pattern is unique. This means that no two zebras have the exact same stripes.

Location

Savanna covers more than half of Africa, mostly in the central and southern parts. These areas have a rainy and a dry season, but it is hot all year.

Giraffe

At up to 19 ft (5.8 m) high, the giraffe is the world's tallest land animal. Its very long neck helps it to reach acacia tree leaves high above the savanna.

Blue wildebeest

The wildebeest looks like a cow, but it is a type of antelope. It travels an astonishing 1,000 miles (1,609 km) every year, just to find the right kind of grass to eat.

Wildebeests are also known as gnus.

Kalahari desert

The Kalahari is a huge, dry, sandy area in southern Africa. In some parts of the Kalahari, it may not rain for up to eight months. Many animals here have to travel in search of fresh grass to eat, and predators follow them.

Sociable weaver

These small birds build giant nests, over 21 ft (6 m) wide, with up to 100 weavers in each one. Some nests are so heavy that they break the tree they're in!

Sociable weavers' massive nests can last for 100 years.

Location

The Kalahari covers most of Botswana and parts of Namibia and South Africa. In summer, it can become as hot as 104°F (40°C).

HABITAT KEY

- Wetlands
- Tropical grasslands
- Scrublands
- Hot desert

SCALE

0 100 miles

0 100 kilometers

ANGOLA

Okavango

Circling high in the desert sky on its broad wings, this bird searches for dead animals to eat.

White-backed vulture

Growing up to 9 ft (2.8 m) tall, the ostrich is the world's largest bird. It can't fly, but it can outrun most of its predators.

Ostrich

This high-leaping antelope moves around in large herds. Both males and females have horns.

Springbok

BOTSWANA

ATLANTIC OCEAN

Windhoek

Warthogs kneel on their front legs when munching on fresh grass.

Common warthog

The aardvark's name means "earth pig." It can eat up to 50,000 ants a night!

Aardvark

During the day, this large rodent sleeps in caves or burrows. At night, it comes out to find plants to eat.

Gaborone

Pretoria

NAMIBIA

N W E S

Cape porcupine

African bullfrog

This big frog lives underground during the dry season, which can last 10 months of each year!

Vaal

Bloemfontein

SOUTH AFRICA

Cheetah

The world's fastest land animal, the cheetah can run at speeds of up to 68 mph (110 kph). It takes just three seconds for this cat to reach its top speed.

Meerkat

Meerkats help each other protect their families. They take turns standing on guard and warn other meerkats if danger approaches.

Madagascar

Madagascar is the fourth-largest island in the world, and it is amazingly rich in wildlife. More than 250,000 different species of animals live here, and two-thirds of them are found nowhere else on Earth. Sadly, many are endangered.

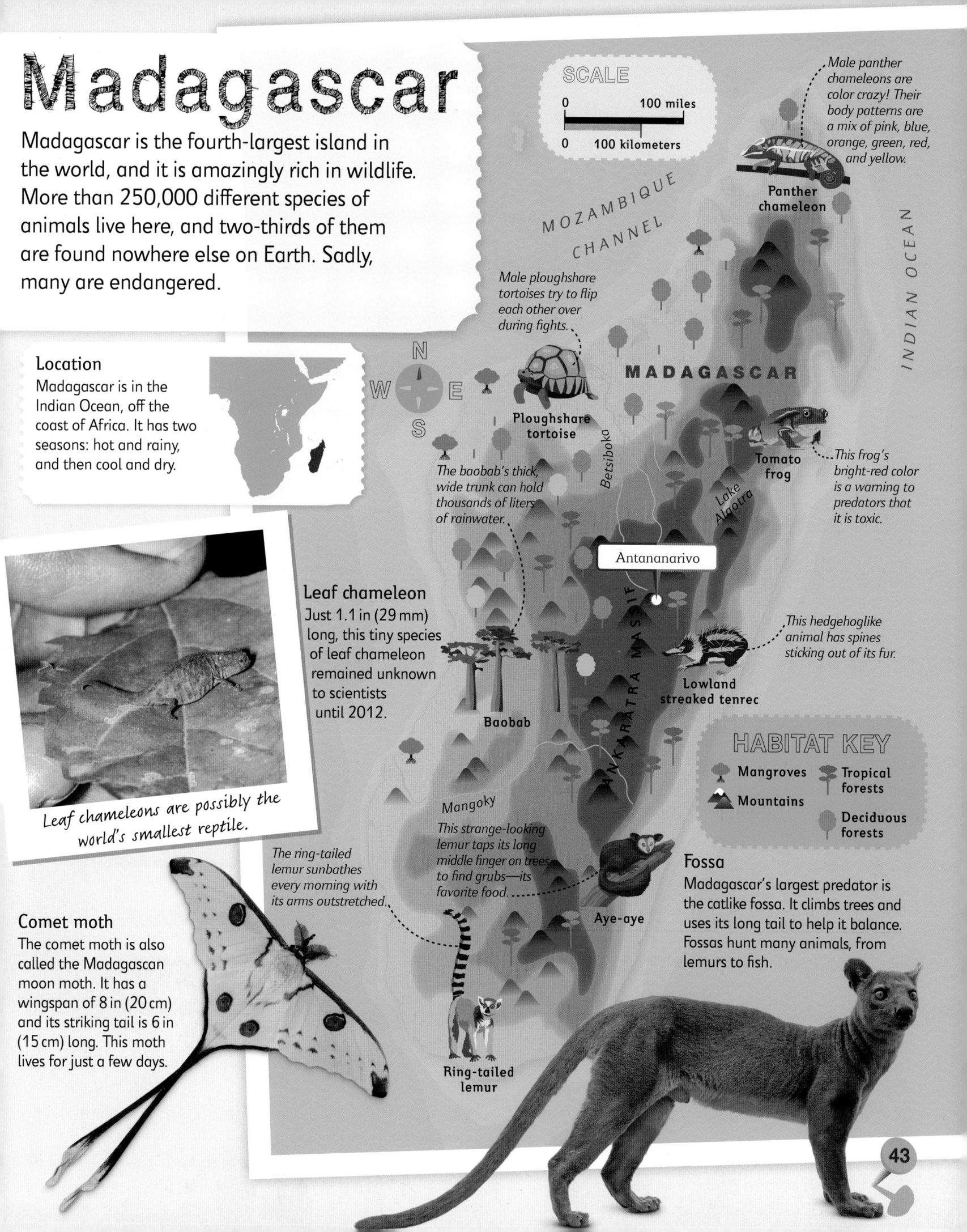

Location

Madagascar is in the Indian Ocean, off the coast of Africa. It has two seasons: hot and rainy, and then cool and dry.

Leaf chameleon

Just 1.1 in (29 mm) long, this tiny species of leaf chameleon remained unknown to scientists until 2012.

Leaf chameleons are possibly the world's smallest reptile.

Comet moth

The comet moth is also called the Madagascan moon moth. It has a wingspan of 8 in (20 cm) and its striking tail is 6 in (15 cm) long. This moth lives for just a few days.

Fossa

Madagascar's largest predator is the catlike fossa. It climbs trees and uses its long tail to help it balance. Fossas hunt many animals, from lemurs to fish.

Kruger National Park

South Africa's Kruger National Park is filled with wildlife. More than 140 mammal species and hundreds of birds live in its savanna, mountains, and tropical forests. Watering holes provide places for animals to drink during the dry season.

Giraffe Special valves in a giraffe's neck stop blood from rushing to its head when it bends over to drink.

Hippopotamus A hippo's eyes, ears, and nose are on top of its head, so it can see, hear, and breathe while the rest of it is underwater.

Honey badger Almost 3 ft (1 m) long, the honey badger is one of the most fearless animals in Africa. It even fights lions!

Aardvark The aardvark uses its wide, strong claws to dig burrows as well as find insects to eat.

The aardvark's nostrils contain lots of hairs to stop dust from going up its nose when it is digging.

The white-backed vulture is the most commonly seen vulture in Africa.

White-backed vulture

This big vulture eats dead animals. Up to 1,000 of them may gather to feed on an elephant carcass, squabbling and fighting while they eat!

Secretary bird

The secretary bird strides through the savanna on its long legs, looking for grasshoppers, voles, and mice to eat. It kills snakes by stomping on them!

Plains zebra Zebra herds travel long distances to find enough grass to eat. They must also drink at least once a day.

African elephant An elephant's trunk contains 40,000 muscles! It uses its trunk to spray water into its mouth for a drink.

African lion In a pride of lions, females do most of the hunting. The male is the only cat with a mane.

Impala To escape predators, impalas leap forward up to 29½ ft (9 m) and as high as 8 ft (2.5 m). Sometimes they leap over each other!

Impalas eat grass in the rainy season and shrubs and herbs at other times.

Bateleur

This eagle's name means "tightrope walker" because it rocks its wings from side to side when it glides, as if it's balancing. Its bright-red face has no feathers at all.

African elephants have much larger ears than Asian elephants.

Location

Kruger National Park covers 7,523 sq miles (19,485 sq km) in northeastern South Africa. It lies south of Zimbabwe and west of Mozambique.

Cheetahs are instantly recognizable from the black spots on their coat.

Cheetah

A cheetah's impressive bursts of speed can only last for short distances. Afterward, it's tired, so other animals can easily steal its kill!

Europe

At first glance, the continent of Europe may seem too crowded for wildlife. There are 739 million people living here, in 44 countries! But with dense forests, sandy beaches, high mountains, and miles of moorland, animals still have plenty of different habitats to choose from.

Scottish moorland

Northern Scotland has acres of moorland. These rainy highlands have acidic, peaty soil, formed by sphagnum moss. They are full of a pretty pink- and purple-flowering shrub called heather. Heather is home to many insects, birds, and small mammals.

The Camargue

This triangular coastal wetland is found where the Rhône River meets the Mediterranean Sea. Its 359 sq miles (930 sq km) of sandy marshes are home to 400 bird species, and to animals unique to this area, such as the Camargue horse.

HABITAT KEY

- Deciduous forests
- Coniferous forests
- Scrublands
- Temperate grasslands
- Deserts
- Tundra
- Ice

ICELAND
ATLANTIC OCEAN
NORWEGIAN SEA
Faroe Islands
Shetland Islands
NORWAY
SWEDEN
NORTH SEA
DENMARK
Bornhol
IRELAND
Isle of Man
UNITED KINGDOM
Channel Islands
NETHERLANDS
BELGIUM
GERMANY
LUXEMBOURG
CZECH REPUBLIC
BAY OF BISCAY
FRANCE
LIECHTENSTEIN
SWITZERLAND
AUSTR
SLOVE
CRO
SAN MARINO
ADRIATIC
ANDORRA
MONACO
ITALY
PORTUGAL
SPAIN
Corsica
Sardinia
VATICAN CITY
Majorca
Minorca
Ibiza
Balearic Islands
TYRRHENIAN SEA
Gibraltar
MEDITERRANEAN SEA
Sicily
MALTA

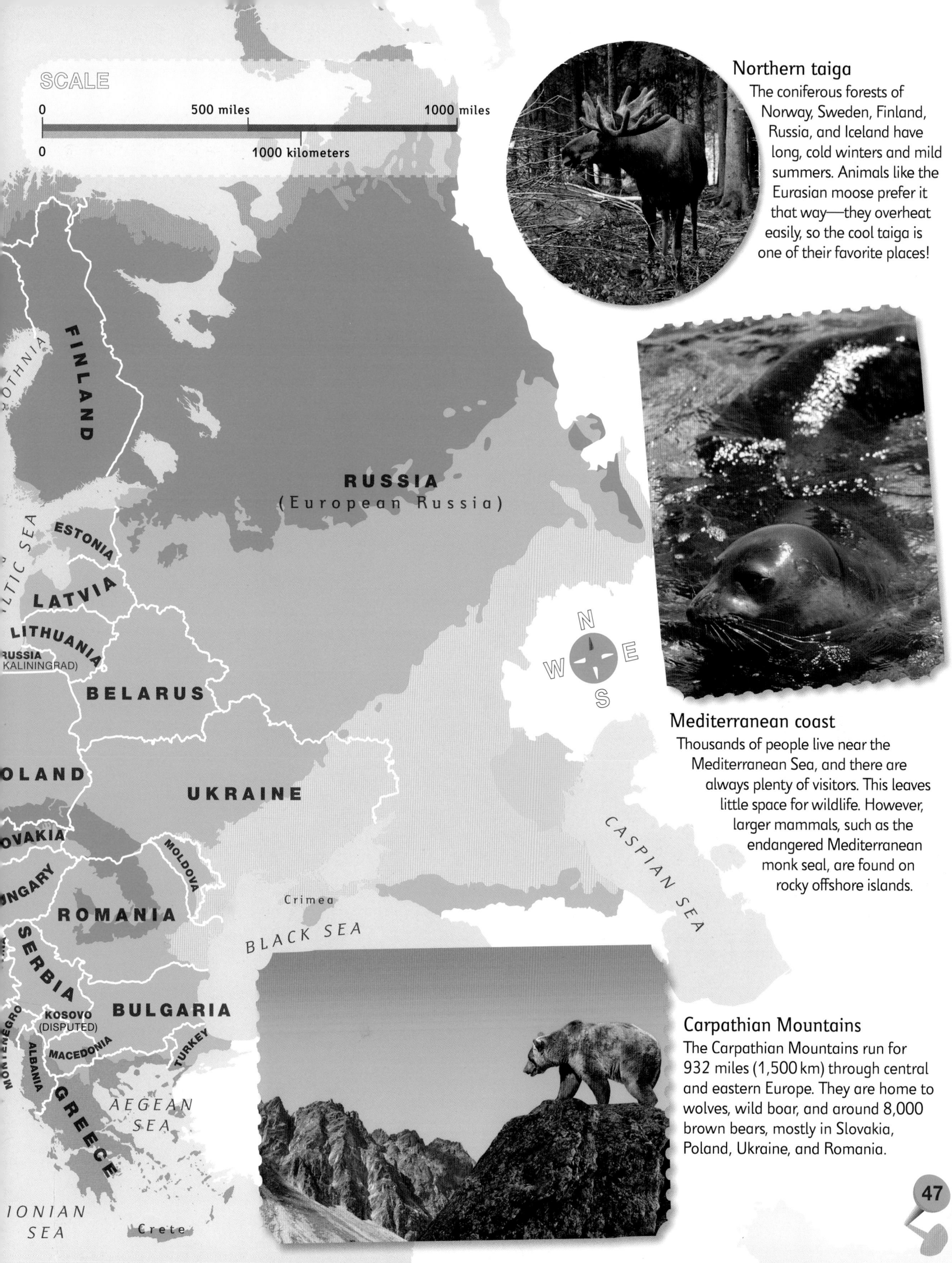

Northern taiga

The coniferous forests of Norway, Sweden, Finland, Russia, and Iceland have long, cold winters and mild summers. Animals like the Eurasian moose prefer it that way—they overheat easily, so the cool taiga is one of their favorite places!

Mediterranean coast

Thousands of people live near the Mediterranean Sea, and there are always plenty of visitors. This leaves little space for wildlife. However, larger mammals, such as the endangered Mediterranean monk seal, are found on rocky offshore islands.

Carpathian Mountains

The Carpathian Mountains run for 932 miles (1,500 km) through central and eastern Europe. They are home to wolves, wild boar, and around 8,000 brown bears, mostly in Slovakia, Poland, Ukraine, and Romania.

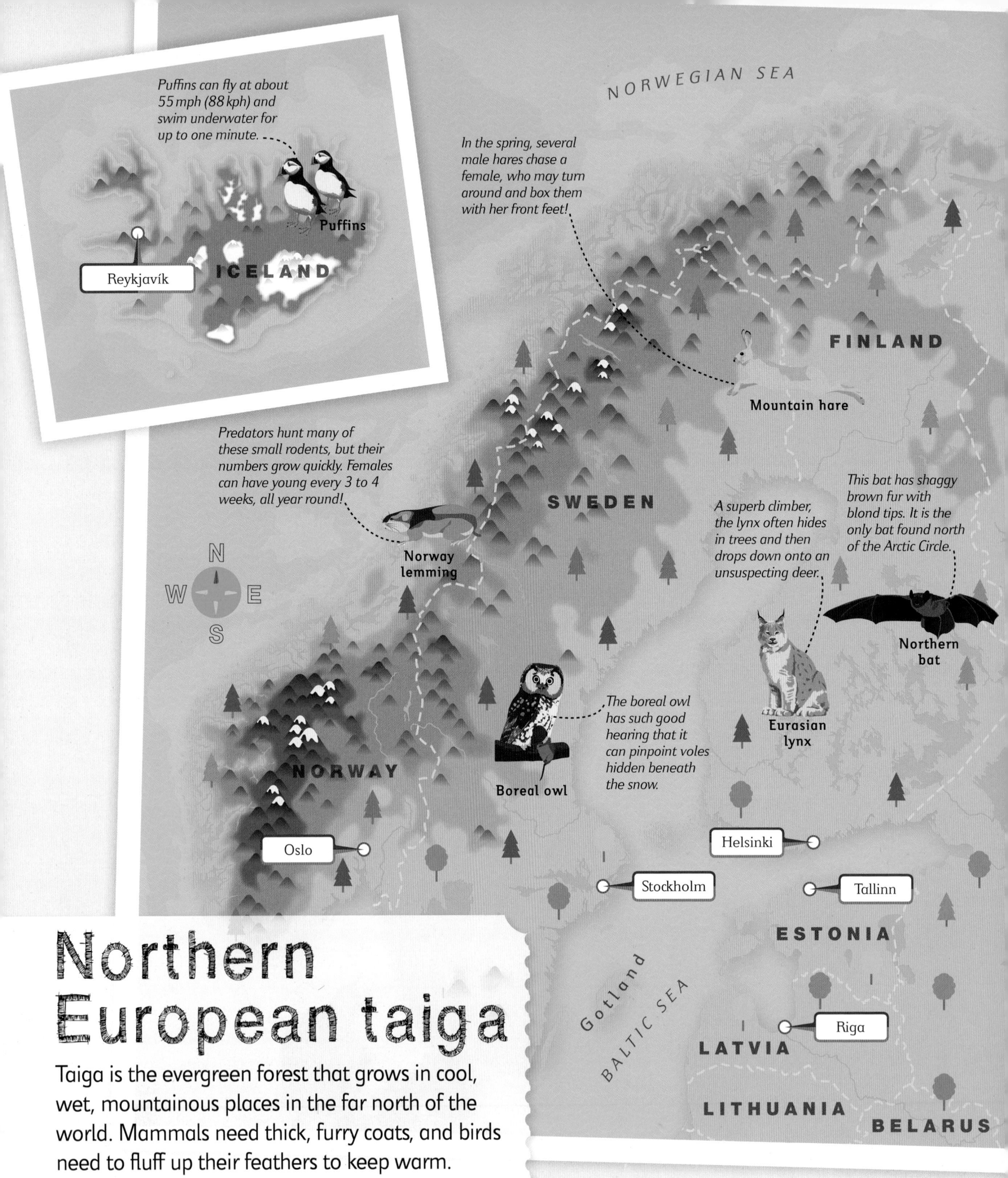

Northern European taiga

Taiga is the evergreen forest that grows in cool, wet, mountainous places in the far north of the world. Mammals need thick, furry coats, and birds need to fluff up their feathers to keep warm. During the cold winters, food can be hard to find.

Carrion crow

The crow has a huge brain for its size. It's so smart that it makes and uses tools, and recognizes faces. It will even teach other crows to identify a mean human!

This type of finch's bill is crossed at the tip, which is ideal for pulling conifer seeds out of cones.

Parrot crossbill

Used as Christmas trees, the Norway spruce can grow to 131 ft (40 m) in height and live for 1,000 years.

Norway spruce

Also called the fish eagle, the osprey plunges into water feetfirst to grab fish with its talons.

Osprey

The wolverine is the biggest member of the weasel family. It has a bite so powerful it can crush bone.

Wolverine

The jay survives cold winters by storing food, especially berries. It hides them in trees, or covers them with bark and lichens.

Siberian jay

Male capercaillies perform a dance in an area called a "lek" to attract females. They put their tails up, their wings down, and make sounds like popping corks!

Western capercaillie

This toad's skin gives off a nasty substance that stops most predators from eating it. It can live for up to 40 years.

Common toad

The eider swallows mussels whole, crushing their shells in its stomach.

Common eider

The eider is the Northern Hemisphere's largest duck. Mother eiders lead their chicks to the sea, where they swim in groups of more than 150 chicks!

Stoat

The stoat is a lightning-fast member of the weasel family. Usually reddish brown, its coat turns white in winter, making it hard to see against the snow. The tip of its tail, however, stays dark.

When a stoat has its white coat, it's called an ermine.

Location

This part of the taiga runs across the top of Europe eastward to the Ural Mountains in western Russia. Winters here are very cold and snowy.

British Isles

The British Isles are made up of the United Kingdom—which includes England, Scotland, Wales, and Northern Ireland—and the Republic of Ireland. Although wolves and bears once lived here, today the largest wild mammal is a deer.

European badger

The badger likes to live in groups. Six or more share a system of underground tunnels called a sett, which they dig out with powerful claws. One badger can eat hundreds of earthworms in a single night!

The European hedgehog has around 5,000 spines in its coat.

European hedgehog

If threatened, this hedgehog curls up into a ball. Although it is known for eating earthworms and slugs, it actually prefers insects—even wasps and bees.

Shetland Islands

Orkney Islands

ATLANTIC OCEAN

N
W E
S

Cold British waters don't bother this marine mammal. It has a 2½ in (6 cm) layer of fat under its skin, called blubber, to keep it warm.

Gray seal

This wildcat looks like a big domestic cat, but it's really a fierce, strong predator with 18 razor-sharp claws!

Scottish wildcat

Red squirrel

Red squirrels can be right- or left-handed—you can tell by the way they handle a pinecone.

Outer Hebrides

Inner Hebrides

GRAMPIANS

Edinburgh

Clyde

Scotland

NORTH SEA

SCALE

0 — 50 miles

0 — 50 kilometers

HABITAT KEY

- Wetlands
- Mountains
- Coniferous forests
- Deciduous forests

Location

This group of islands is found off the northwest coast of mainland Europe. The weather is often wet and windy, but summers can also be very warm.

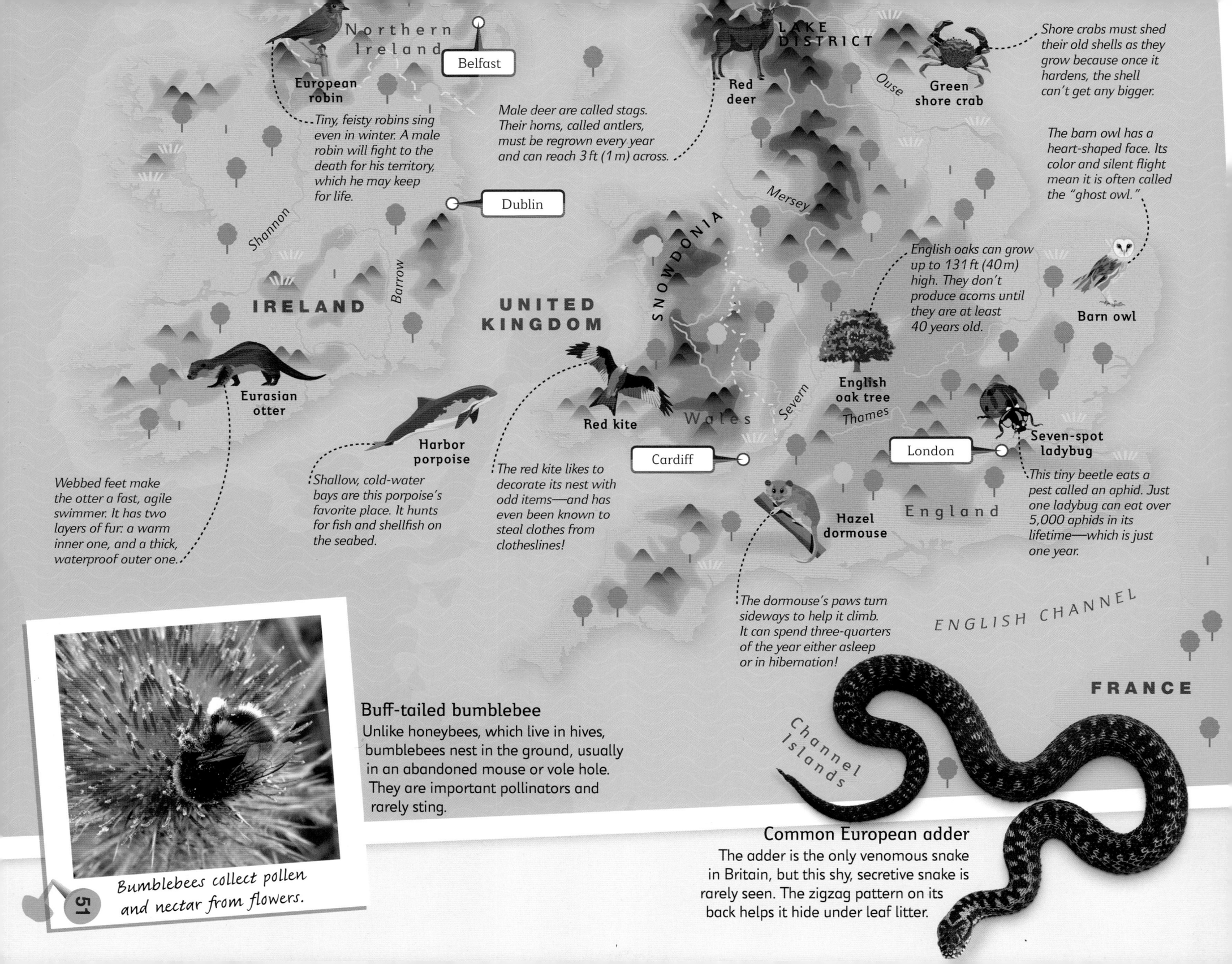
Northern Ireland
Belfast
European robin
Tiny, feisty robins sing even in winter. A male robin will fight to the death for his territory, which he may keep for life.
Male deer are called stags. Their horns, called antlers, must be regrown every year and can reach 3 ft (1 m) across.
LAKE DISTRICT
Red deer
Ouse
Green shore crab
Shore crabs must shed their old shells as they grow because once it hardens, the shell can't get any bigger.
The barn owl has a heart-shaped face. Its color and silent flight mean it is often called the "ghost owl."
Dublin
Shannon
Barrow
Mersey
SNOWDONIA
IRELAND
UNITED KINGDOM
English oaks can grow up to 131 ft (40 m) high. They don't produce acorns until they are at least 40 years old.
Barn owl
Eurasian otter
Harbor porpoise
Red kite
Wales
Severn
English oak tree
Thames
Seven-spot ladybug
London
Cardiff
Webbed feet make the otter a fast, agile swimmer. It has two layers of fur: a warm inner one, and a thick, waterproof outer one.
Shallow, cold-water bays are this porpoise's favorite place. It hunts for fish and shellfish on the seabed.
The red kite likes to decorate its nest with odd items—and has even been known to steal clothes from clotheslines!
Hazel dormouse
England
This tiny beetle eats a pest called an aphid. Just one ladybug can eat over 5,000 aphids in its lifetime—which is just one year.
The dormouse's paws turn sideways to help it climb. It can spend three-quarters of the year either asleep or in hibernation!
ENGLISH CHANNEL
FRANCE
Channel Islands
Bumblebees collect pollen and nectar from flowers.
Buff-tailed bumblebee
Unlike honeybees, which live in hives, bumblebees nest in the ground, usually in an abandoned mouse or vole hole. They are important pollinators and rarely sting.
Common European adder
The adder is the only venomous snake in Britain, but this shy, secretive snake is rarely seen. The zigzag pattern on its back helps it hide under leaf litter.

European forests

Forests here mostly have a mix of trees. Some, like the Bavarian Forest in Germany, have more conifers, such as spruce. Others, such as Białoweża Forest in Poland, have more broad-leaved trees, like oak. All, however, provide great homes for animals.

NORWAY
Oslo
Stockholm
FINLAND
BALTIC SEA
SWEDEN
Copenhagen
DENMARK
LATVIA
LITHUAN

This little rodent doesn't hibernate in winter. Instead, it moves around beneath the snow, searching for plants to eat.

Bank vole

Families of blue tits gather together in winter to search for food. They eat insects in the summer, but eat seeds in the winter.

A wood ant colony contains around 250,000 workers. This ant can spray formic acid to keep enemies away!

The Hague
NETHERLANDS
GERMANY
Amsterdam
Berlin
Warsaw
London
BRITISH ISLES
Brussels
BELGIUM
LUXEMBOURG
Eurasian blue tit
Red wood ant
POLAND

This millipede might look scary, but it is actually a vegetarian—it eats rotting plants.

This insect gets its name from the male's jaws, which look like the antlers of a male deer, or stag. Males get up to 3 in (7.5 cm) long.

Nightjars live in Africa in the winter, but return to Europe to nest in the spring. Their speckled feathers hide them perfectly among dead leaves.

Prague
CZECH REPUBLIC
Paris
Black millipede
SLOVAKIA
LICHTENSTEIN
Vienna
Bratislava
AUSTRIA
European nightjar
Bern
Budapest
FRANCE
SWITZERLAND
Stag beetle
SLOVENIA
HUNGARY
ROMANIA
Ljubljana
Zagreb
CROATIA
SERBIA

This mink is one of Europe's most endangered mammals. It lives near rivers and streams, and hunts mostly at night.

European mink

Belgrade
BOSNIA & HERZEGOVINA
MONACO
SAN MARINO
Sarajevo
Pristina
Sofia
ANDORRA
VATICAN CITY
MONTENEGRO
Podgorica
KOSOVO
Skopje
Rome
ITALY
Tirana
MACEDONIA
ALBANIA
MEDITERRANEAN SEA
GREECE

A red fox's bushy tail is called a brush.

Red fox

This adaptable mammal can live almost anywhere—farms or city centers, marshes or mountaintops. It lives in more places in the world than any other carnivore.

Location

There are areas of forest in mainland Europe from Portugal as far as Russia. Some get really hot in summer, while others are cool all year round.

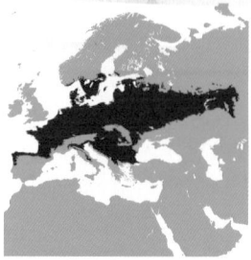

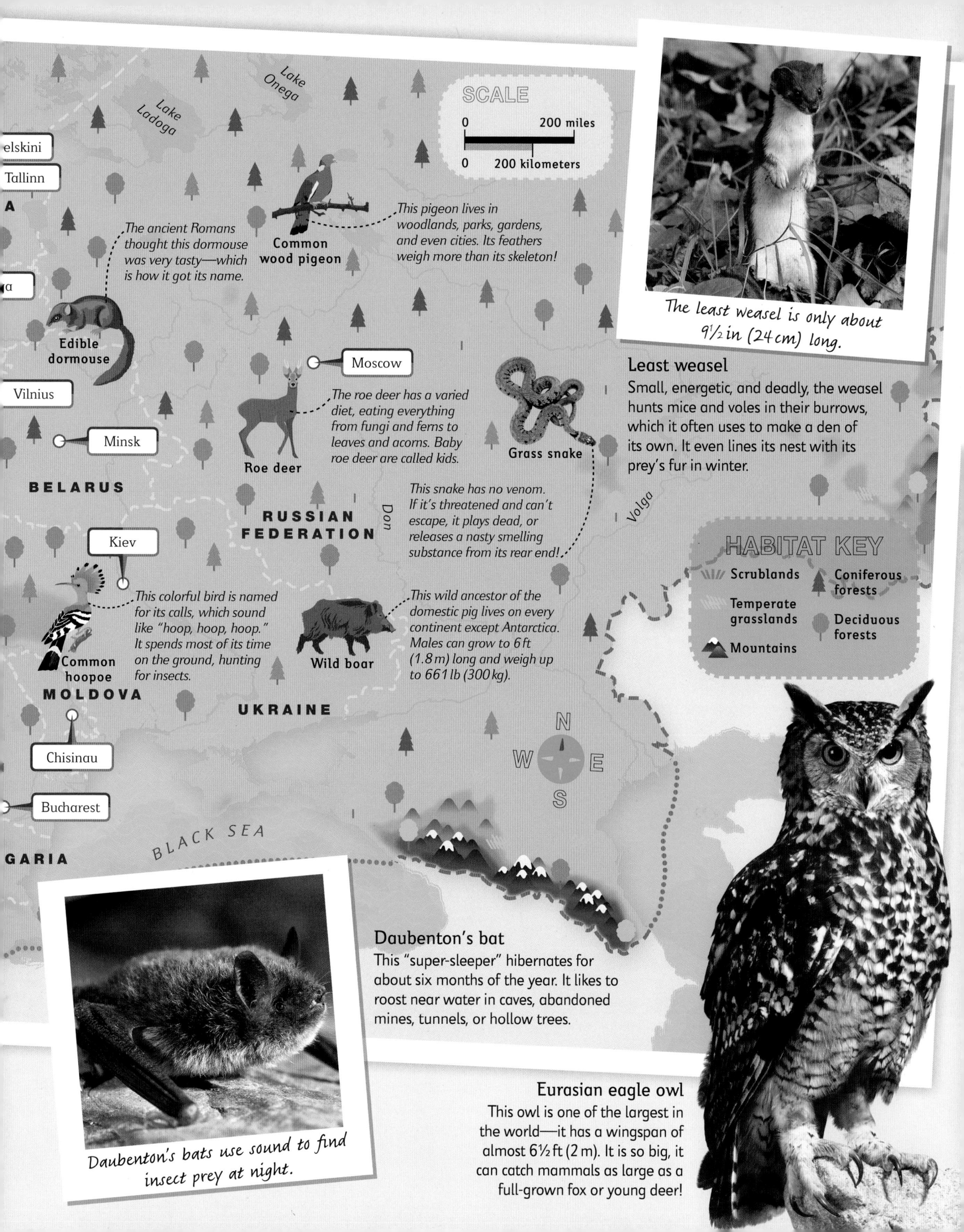
Lake Onega
Lake Ladoga
elskini
Tallinn
A
a
Vilnius
Minsk
BELARUS
Moscow
RUSSIAN FEDERATION
Don
Volga
Kiev
MOLDOVA
Chisinau
Bucharest
GARIA
UKRAINE
BLACK SEA
SCALE
0 200 miles
0 200 kilometers
Common wood pigeon
This pigeon lives in woodlands, parks, gardens, and even cities. Its feathers weigh more than its skeleton!
The ancient Romans thought this dormouse was very tasty—which is how it got its name.
Edible dormouse
Roe deer
The roe deer has a varied diet, eating everything from fungi and ferns to leaves and acorns. Baby roe deer are called kids.
Grass snake
This snake has no venom. If it's threatened and can't escape, it plays dead, or releases a nasty smelling substance from its rear end!
Common hoopoe
This colorful bird is named for its calls, which sound like "hoop, hoop, hoop." It spends most of its time on the ground, hunting for insects.
Wild boar
This wild ancestor of the domestic pig lives on every continent except Antarctica. Males can grow to 6 ft (1.8 m) long and weigh up to 661 lb (300 kg).
HABITAT KEY
Scrublands
Coniferous forests
Temperate grasslands
Deciduous forests
Mountains
N
W
E
S
The least weasel is only about 9½ in (24 cm) long.
Least weasel
Small, energetic, and deadly, the weasel hunts mice and voles in their burrows, which it often uses to make a den of its own. It even lines its nest with its prey's fur in winter.
Daubenton's bat
This "super-sleeper" hibernates for about six months of the year. It likes to roost near water in caves, abandoned mines, tunnels, or hollow trees.
Daubenton's bats use sound to find insect prey at night.
Eurasian eagle owl
This owl is one of the largest in the world—it has a wingspan of almost 6½ ft (2 m). It is so big, it can catch mammals as large as a full-grown fox or young deer!

The Alps

The mountains of the Alps divide the cooler northern parts of Europe from the warm southern parts. With mountain lakes, glaciers, meadows, and forests, there are plenty of places for different animals to live. As many as 30,000 different species make their home here.

Location

The Alps stretch through eight countries in total. The highest parts are always snowy, but in summer lower parts can reach 86°F (30°C).

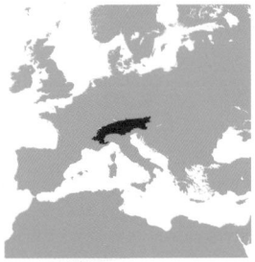

Young shrews "caravan" behind their mother, by following each other in a line, holding onto the shrew in front by their mouth!

This hoofed mammal is able to run up to 31 mph (50 kph), even on a snow-covered mountain!

GERMANY

N W E S

LICHTENSTEIN

SWITZERLAND

AUSTRIA

FRANCE

Alpine shrew

Chamois

SLOVENIA

Bern

Ljubljana

This ptarmigan turns white in the winter to hide from predators in the snow.

Rock ptarmigan

Alpine chough

Apollo butterfly

The endangered Apollo butterfly's bright-red wing spots fade in the sun, so older butterflies have spots that are more orange.

Built for flight, the alpine chough has been seen soaring as high as 26,250 ft (8,000 m) above sea level!

CROATIA

ITALY

Alpine ibex

The sure-footed ibex has long curved horns that grow up to 40 in (100 cm) long in males.

SCALE

0 — 100 miles

0 — 100 kilometers

HABITAT KEY

Scrublands

Mountains

Coniferous forests

Deciduous forests

Alpine salamander

Although it mostly comes out at night, this little black salamander also ventures out in the daytime after rain.

Pine marten

Powerful forelimbs and strong claws make martens excellent climbers. They even race through the trees to hunt squirrels.

Alpine marmot

The alpine marmot digs long, deep burrows where it hibernates for up to nine months of the year. When hibernating, a marmot breathes just one to two times a minute!

The marmot lives in high alpine meadows and pastures.

European steppe

The steppe is a temperate grassland habitat. Many animals here are seasonal visitors from other habitats, while some, such as hamsters and moles, live here all year round.

Black-bellied hamster

This hamster digs summer and fall burrows 19½ in (50 cm) below the ground's surface. Its winter burrow can be 6½ ft (2 m) deep. When swimming, this hamster inflates its cheek pouches to act like water wings!

Black fur on its underside gives the black-bellied hamster its name.

RUSSIAN FEDERATION

SCALE
0 200 miles
0 200 kilometers

Minsk

BELARUS

Kiev

UKRAINE

ROMANIA

Bucharest

BULGARIA

Sofia

MACEDONIA

N
W E
S

This pink and black starling eats locusts and other grasshoppers it finds on the steppe.

Rosy starling

The colorful marbled polecat travels up to 0.6 miles (1 km) a night searching for food.

Marbled polecat

Golden eagle

This big bird of prey can live for up to 32 years. It makes a nest, called an aerie, in a tall tree or on a cliff ledge.

Although they each have their own burrow, there might be 6,000 giant mole rats in just 0.4 sq miles (1 sq km) of grassland!

The mole's big forepaws are always turned outward to help it dig its underground tunnels.

European mole

Great bustard

This is the heaviest flying bird on Earth. Males weigh up to 35 lb (16 kg)!

Harvest mouse

Weighing just 0.2 oz (6 g), the tiny harvest mouse is Europe's smallest rodent.

Giant mole rat

HABITAT KEY

- Scrublands
- Mountains
- Coniferous forests
- Deciduous forests

Location

The European steppe stretches from Romania in the west to the Ural Mountains in the east, where it merges with the Asian steppe.

Only males have a crest on their backs.

Common nightingale

This little bird is plain to look at, but its song sets it apart. Nightingale songs have high and low notes, phrases, and trills that other birds can't make.

Northern crested newt

Also called the great crested newt, this amphibian gets up to 6½ in (17 cm) long. Newts are most active at night, and spend the day hiding in ponds, or under damp logs or rocks.

Mediterranean scrubland

The coastal areas around the Mediterranean Sea contain rocky hills and flat, shrub-filled plains. This rare habitat is found in only a few places on Earth. Plants here can survive wildfires, and animals have to deal with hot, dry weather.

Mediterranean chameleon

This is one of only two chameleon species found in Europe. Its tongue is sticky to catch passing insects. It is also twice the length of its body!

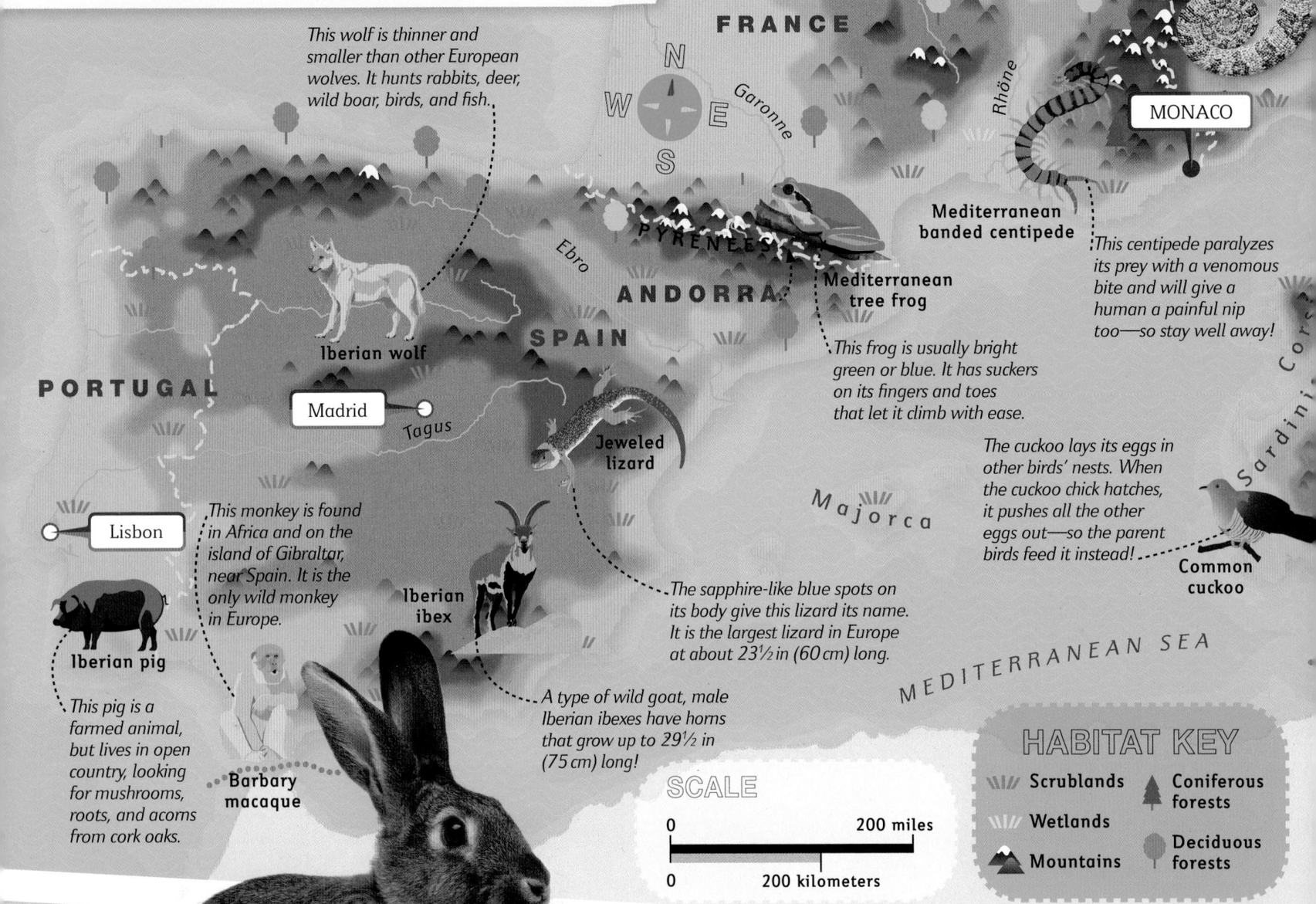

European rabbit

The European rabbit is the ancestor of all pet rabbits in the world. Unlike its enemy, the Iberian lynx, the rabbit has been seen in yards and parks, and even in busy cities.

Location

This region includes the southern parts of Europe around the Mediterranean Sea, as well as islands like Crete that share a similar habitat.

The hawk moth will return to a nectar-rich flower day after day.

Hummingbird hawk moth

This insect beats its wings so fast that they make a humming sound—just like the birds it's named after. It feeds on nectar made by flowers like buddleia and honeysuckle.

Iberian lynx

Just 404 adult Iberian lynxes are left in the wild, so this is the most endangered cat on Earth—but the good news is this figure is nearly twice the number of wild lynxes alive a few years ago!

The Iberian lynx mostly hunts just one animal—the European rabbit.

Zagreb
CROATIA
Golden jackal
SAN MARINO
The golden jackal is found in many places, including southeastern Europe, northern Africa, and southern Asia.
Belgrade
ROMANIA
BOSNIA & HERZEGOVINA
ITALY
Sarajevo
SERBIA
MONTENEGRO
Pristina
Rome
VATICAN CITY
Podgorica
KOSOVO
ADRIATIC SEA
The cork oak is one of few trees that can grow new bark. The cork bark is harvested once every nine years to make bottle stoppers and other items.
Skopje
BULGARIA
Tirana
MACEDONIA
ALBANIA
Cork oak
Dalmatian pelican
GREECE
The magpie is so smart that it can make and use tools. It eats insects and seeds, and will even steal other birds' eggs.
In addition to making other sounds, this pelican barks and hisses! When fishing, it fills up its beak with food to eat later.
Eurasian magpie
Marginated tortoise
Sicily
This plant-eating tortoise lives mostly in Greece, in thorny, rocky, scrubby areas.
Athens
MEDITERRANEAN SEA
MALTA
Crete

Mediterranean house gecko

This little gecko is about 4 in (10 cm) long and weighs about as much as a sugar cube. It is also called a "moon lizard" because it mostly comes out at night. It eats small cockroaches and moths.

Białowieża Forest

Białowieża is lowland Europe's only old-growth, or "primeval," forest. Forests like this once covered all of northeastern Europe. Its many different trees and habitats mean Białowieża is home to thousands of animals, including the rare European bison!

Red deer Red deer find leaves, small twigs, and bark to eat in the fall and winter, and herbs and grasses during the summer.

Pine marten Pine martens are related to weasels but, unlike weasels, they hunt in the trees. They chase small mammals such as squirrels.

Red fox Foxes feed on a wide variety of foods. In Białowieża, they eat yellow-necked mice, hares, and the carcasses of red deer killed by wolves or lynxes.

A male and female red fox have a territory that they share, which is where they raise their young.

All domestic dogs are descended from the gray wolf.

Gray wolf

The gray wolf is found in Europe, North America, and Asia. Packs of four to five wolves hunt deer, elk, wild boar, rabbits, and beavers.

Common toad

Many parts of this forest are wet, including rare places known as "spruce bog forests," where coniferous spruce trees grow in very wet ground. These habitats make a perfect home for the common toad!

Great spotted woodpecker Woodpeckers nest in holes made in tree trunks. They search for tasty insect prey in the bark.

European bison The bison is Europe's largest land mammal. There are around 900 in Białowieża forest.

Tawny owl This woodland owl hunts at night for birds, rodents, amphibians such as frogs, and bats to eat.

Yellow-necked mouse This mouse prefers living in woodland, because it eats a lot of tree seeds. It is also an excellent tree climber!

Eurasian red squirrel Eurasian red squirrels like to eat seeds, especially from conifer trees.

Eurasian badger Badgers are common in forests. In addition to plenty of worms to eat, they find lots of hollow trees, which they use as daytime shelters.

Old-growth forests have plenty of standing dead trees as well as live ones. Woodpecker nests or holes where the tree has rotted make ideal bat roosts.

Noctule bat

Noctule bats nest in hollow trees. The holes must be high enough to avoid predators such as pine martens. Noctules are one of the first bats to come out at night, and hunt moths and flying ants.

Location

Białowieża Forest covers 579 sq miles (1,500 sq km) across Poland and Belarus. Temperatures range from 21°F (-6°C) in winter to 75°F (24°C) in summer.

Beavers produce an oily substance that keeps their fur waterproof.

Eurasian beaver

The Eurasian beaver disappeared from Białowieża in the mid-19th century due to hunting. It was reintroduced in 1956. Today, they live all along the rivers, streams, and ponds throughout the forest.

Asia

Welcome to Earth's largest continent! Asia contains half the world's human population, but there is still a lot of land for wildlife. Habitats here include vast deserts, grassy plains, snowy mountains, and dense, green rain forests.

Savanna

This region in northern India is warm all year round. It has the highest grasslands in the world—some grow more than 10 ft (3 m) tall! The grasslands provide food for deer and rhinos, and cover for predators such as the tiger.

City wildlife

The Turkish capital of Istanbul is rich in wildlife—337 of the country's 483 bird species, such as this seagull, live here. The city is also part of an important migration route for hundreds of thousands of storks, raptors, and water birds each year.

MEDITERRANEAN SEA
BLACK SEA
CASPIAN SEA
RED SEA
GULF OF ADEN
ARABIAN SEA
BAY O
TURKEY
CYPRUS
GEORGIA
ARMENIA
AZERBAIJAN
KAZAKHSTAN
UZBEKISTAN
TURKMENISTAN
KYRGYZSTAN
TAJIKISTAN
AFGHANISTAN
LEBANON
SYRIA
ISRAEL
JORDAN
IRAQ
IRAN
KUWAIT
SAUDI ARABIA
BAHRAIN
QATAR
UNITED ARAB EMIRATES
PAKISTAN
NEP
OMAN
YEMEN
Socotra
INDIA
SRI LANKA
Maldives
INDIA
N
W
E
S

Arabian highlands

The Arabian highlands are made of the mountains and high plateaus that border the desert of the Arabian Peninsula, in southwest Asia. The highlands are cooler than the desert, and have more rainfall, so shrubs and grasses can grow. These plants are food for animals such as camels.

Himalayas

Running through northeast India and parts of five other Asian countries, the Himalayas are the world's highest mountains. Their highest, rockiest areas offer enough food sources for the rare snow leopard, and this strong yak.

Bornean rain forest

Borneo is the third-biggest island in the world, and the Bornean rain forest is 140 million years old! About 221 mammal species live here, including Asia's only great ape, the highly endangered orangutan.

Russian taiga

Taiga is also called "snow forest." It's found in cool, high places, like in northeast Russia, and is made up of coniferous forests. Animals use trees for food and shelter, and as places to hide from predators.

Brown bear

The most widespread of all bear species, the brown bear eats mostly roots, berries, and other parts of plants, but it will also hunt animals. Adults can be more than 7 ft (2 m) tall when they stand on their hind legs.

A brown bear takes to the river to hunt for salmon.

Siberian tiger

This is the world's biggest wild cat. Males weigh up to 660 lb (300 kg). It even has a mane, like a lion's, to help keep its neck warm in cold Siberian winters.

Ural owl

This big owl hunts rodents, frogs, and birds that it spots from its perch. In spring, it sings a courtship duet with its lifelong mate.

The Ural owl aggressively defends its territory, chasing away intruders.

Location

Taiga stretches over northeast Russia, eastward to the Pacific Ocean. Summers are short, but the winters are long and snowy.

Black woodpecker

Strong neck muscles and a sharp bill make this bird a champion wood borer. It chisels out holes in tree trunks, where it lays its eggs.

Asian steppe

A steppe is a high, grassy, mostly treeless plain. Animals here live on grass and other plants—or on the animals that do! They must be able to survive freezing winters, hot summers, and harsh wind, and to go long periods without water. On the steppe, watering holes are in short supply.

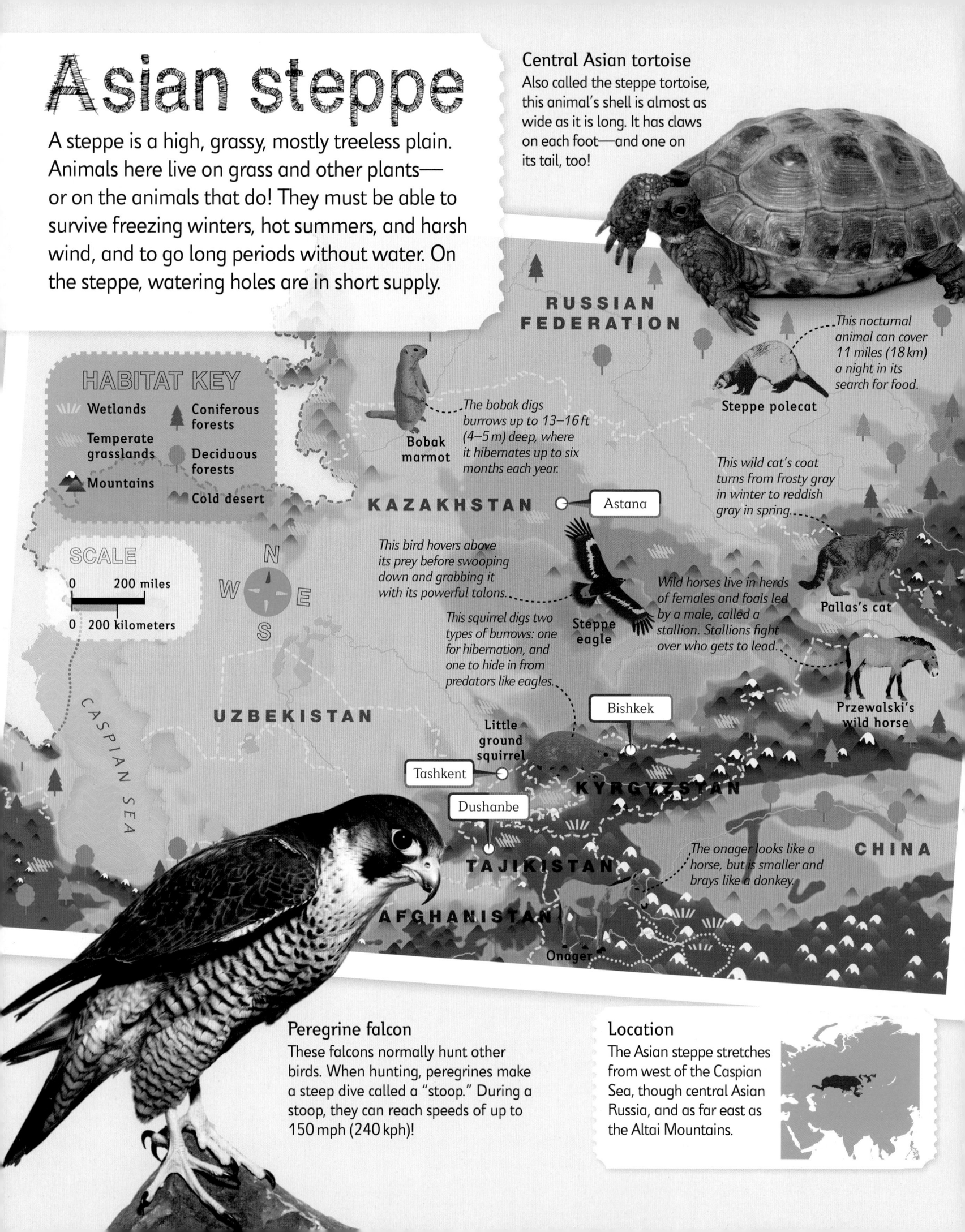

Central Asian tortoise

Also called the steppe tortoise, this animal's shell is almost as wide as it is long. It has claws on each foot—and one on its tail, too!

Peregrine falcon

These falcons normally hunt other birds. When hunting, peregrines make a steep dive called a "stoop." During a stoop, they can reach speeds of up to 150 mph (240 kph)!

Location

The Asian steppe stretches from west of the Caspian Sea, though central Asian Russia, and as far east as the Altai Mountains.

A secret toadhead agama stands alert.

Secret toadhead agama

The insect-eating agama keeps several secrets. It may look like a regular desert lizard, but when it displays, it opens its mouth to reveal a deep reddish pink and expands two spiny cheek flaps.

Location

There are deserts in Kazakhstan, Uzbekistan, and Turkmenistan, and parts of Afghanistan, Pakistan, and Iran.

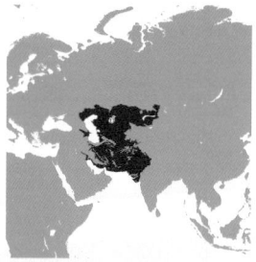

When a predator is near, this hedgehog growls and hisses like a cat, then rolls itself into a protective ball.

Astana

Long-eared hedgehog

The corsac fox uses its long, wide ears to listen for rodent noises in the desert.

Corsac fox

KAZAKHSTAN

SCALE

0 200 miles

0 200 kilometers

N W E S

At up to 13 in (33 cm) long, this is the largest gerbil on Earth.

Great gerbil

Bishkek

Tashkent

KYRGYZSTAN

UZBEKISTAN

This is the world's most venomous true cobra. Though it lives in the desert, it is very good at swimming.

Central Asian cobra

This hare comes out at night to feed on desert plants. It rests in a shallow scrape in the ground during the day.

Yerevan

AZERBAIJAN

TURKMENISTAN

CHINA

ARMENIA

Baku

Dushanbe

TAJIKISTAN

The wild goat lives in dry, rocky areas. Its curved horns have a very sharp inside edge.

Ashgabat

Tolai hare

Tehran

Kabul

Wild goat

Islamabad

Tehran

IRAN

AFGHANISTAN

Baghdad

PAKISTAN

Goitered gazelle

A big, swollen tube on its throat gives this gazelle its name. It also gives males an extra-loud voice.

HABITAT KEY

- Wetlands
- Temperate grasslands
- Mountains
- Cold desert
- Hot desert
- Coniferous forests
- Deciduous forests
- Tropical forests

Central Asian deserts

There are different kinds of deserts here. Some are salty and sandy. Others are rocky or have clay soil. All are dry. Water is found mostly near desert borders where rivers can overflow.

Tibetan Plateau

This high, flat region of Asia is surrounded by mountains. It's so high that it's often called the "roof of the world." The animals that live here have to deal with thin air and bitter winters.

Location

This region includes Tibet and parts of southwest China. Summers are dry and warm, and winters are often below freezing.

Asiatic black bear

This bear is also called the "moon bear" due to the pale, crescent-shaped band on its chest. It spends about half of its life up in trees.

HABITAT KEY

- Coniferous forests
- Mountains
- Cold desert
- Deciduous forests

Many kinds of plants grow on the plateau, including this serratula, a type of thistle.

Himalayan alpine serratula

This large, cowlike animal has extra-big lungs that help it to get enough oxygen from the thin air.

Wild yak

This little relative of the rabbit is so suited to rocky ground that it often nests in a pile of stones!

Himalayan mouse hare

PAKISTAN

The tahr is a wild goat that has hooves with rubberlike cores. These help it grip onto smooth rocks.

Himalayan tahr

HIMALAYAS

NEPAL

INDIA

N W E S

Himalayan wolf

The Himalayan wolf is a rare type of gray wolf. Some are almost white—like snow on the Himalayas!

Himalayan marmots dig very deep burrows to hibernate in.

Himalayan marmot

Nicknamed the "Tibetan snow pig," this ground squirrel is one of the only mammals on Earth that lives above 16,400 ft (5,000 m).

SCALE
0 100 miles
0 100 kilometers
TIAN SHAN
CHINA
BHUTAN
MYANMAR
BANGLADESH
Mountain weasel
When threatened, the mountain weasel scares away predators with a foul-smelling spray called musk.
Bearded vulture
This bird picks up bones in its claws and carries them high into the air. It then drops the bones on rocks to shatter them into bite-sized pieces.
Pandas are the only bears that eat just plants.
Giant panda
The giant panda lives in six forests in central China. It spends 10 to 16 hours a day eating mostly bamboo, and sleeps the rest of the time.
Chiru
The chiru is a type of antelope. It has soft wool, called shahtoosh, which is very good at keeping it warm through winter.
Bharal
Also called the Himalayan blue sheep, the bharal has a bluish sheen to its gray coat. This makes it hard for its enemies to see it against rocky cliffs.
Tibetan sand fox
This very rare fox hunts rodents and lizards. Its slitlike eyes help to lessen glare from the sun.
Kiang
Herds of kiang can have as many as 400 animals. When they travel, kiangs follow their female leader in single file.
Red panda
This raccoonlike animal is also called the "fire fox" or "fire cat" due to its striking red fur.
Tibetan toad
This toad is one of the very few amphibians that are able to live so high up.
Snow leopard
These cats have a thick, spotted coat that keeps them warm and helps them blend in when hunting. They keep their face warm when they sleep by covering it with their furry tail.

East Asian forests

Eastern Asia's deciduous forests are full of trees like oak and ash, as well as some walnut and birch. With streams and rivers, mountains and grassland edges, they are a haven for animals.

A Chinese peacock butterfly feeds on a spider lily plant.

Chinese peacock butterfly

This forest butterfly's size depends on what time of the year it comes out of its cocoon. Spring Chinese peacocks have a wingspan of up to 3 in (8 cm). Summer ones have a wingspan up to 5 in (12 cm).

Japanese sika deer

The sika is a small deer—males are only 3 ft (95 cm) at shoulder height. They make strange noises, too, such as the male's long, whistlelike call that sounds like a siren.

YABLONOI MOUNTAINS

Ulan Bator

MONGOLIA

GOBI DESERT

Beijing

This snake eats poisonous toads, absorbs the poisons, then releases them later from its neck glands!

Asian tiger keelback

This monkey has a blue face! It spends 95 percent of its time in the trees.

Golden snub-nosed monkey

Huang He

Male Baikal teals make a deep chuckling sound—wot-wot-wot!

Baikal teal

CHINA

Yangtze

Earth's largest amphibian grows to 6 ft (1.8 m) long. That's longer than many adult humans are tall!

Chinese giant salamander

This is the smallest of the "big cats." Cloudlike spots help this leopard blend in with its forest home.

Clouded leopard

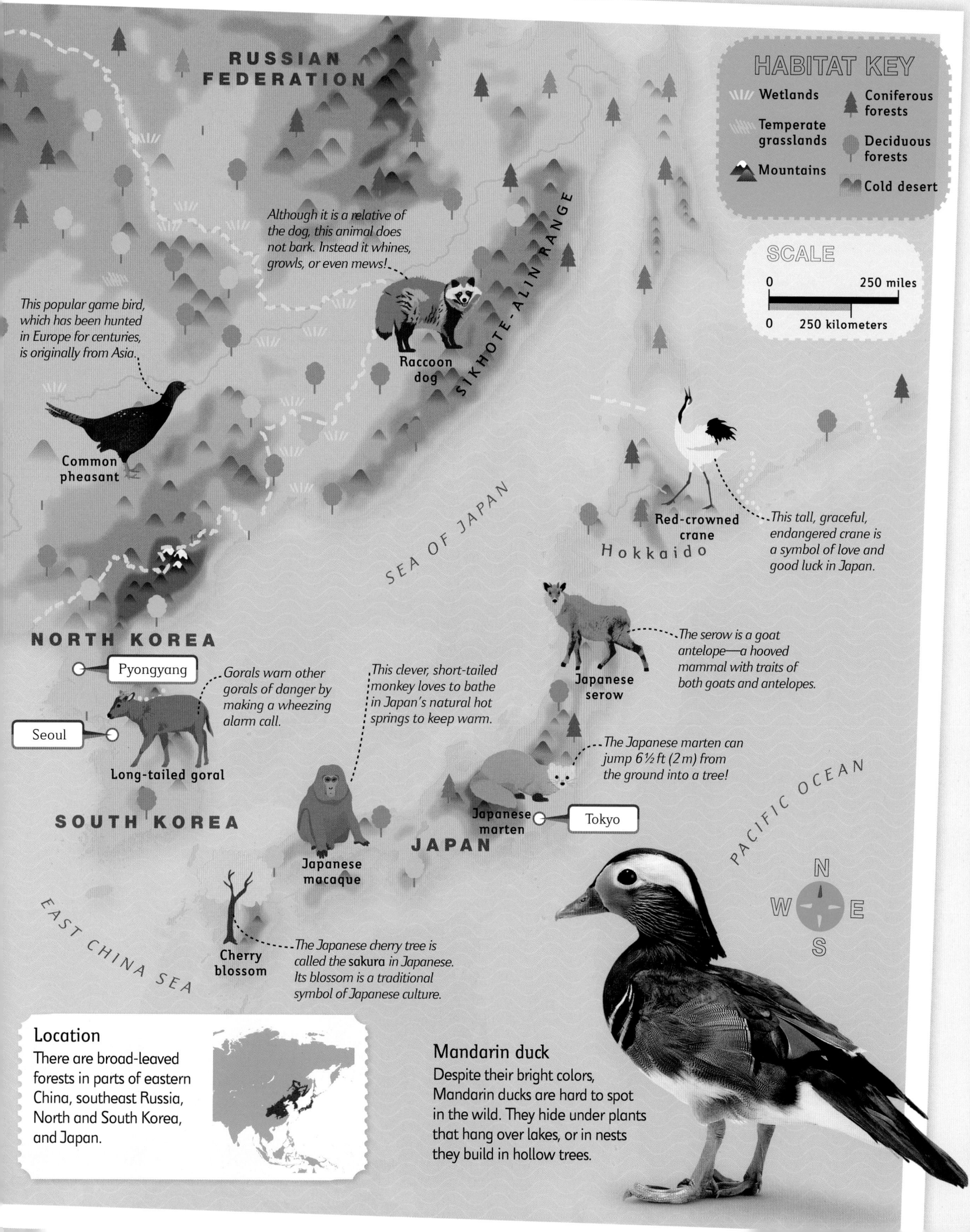

Location

There are broad-leaved forests in parts of eastern China, southeast Russia, North and South Korea, and Japan.

Mandarin duck

Despite their bright colors, Mandarin ducks are hard to spot in the wild. They hide under plants that hang over lakes, or in nests they build in hollow trees.

Arabian Peninsula

The Arabian Peninsula is a hot, dry part of the world, and it is covered by sandy deserts. The animals that live here have special ways of dealing with its harsh conditions.

Arabian partridge

This partridge lives on the ground, where it looks for seeds, grass, and insects to eat. The female lays her eggs in a shallow, scooped-out hole.

Partridges run rather than fly away when threatened.

JORDAN

ISRAEL

IRAQ

IRAN

BAHRAIN

QATAR

UNITED ARAB EMIRATES

SAUDI ARABIA

OMAN

YEMEN

RED SEA

N W E S

Riyadh

Muscat

Sana'a

Location

Located between Africa and Asia, the Arabian Peninsula is made up of Saudi Arabia and several smaller countries.

SCALE

0 200 miles

0 200 kilometers

HABITAT KEY

Wetlands

Mountains

Deciduous forests

Hot desert

Caracal

This cat can jump 10 ft (3 m) off the ground to snatch birds out of the air.

Arabian oryx

Spadelike hooves let this antelope walk on the soft desert sand with ease.

Arabian horse

People of the desert, called the Bedouin, bred this horse to be fast, strong, and able to withstand desert conditions.

Sand cat

Fur on the bottom of its feet helps the sand cat walk over hot ground.

Mountain gazelle

Male gazelles have "air-cushion" fights—they charge at each other but stop just before they crash.

Sandfish

The sandfish is a type of lizard that "swims" beneath the surface of the sand using its flipperlike feet.

Arabian camel spider

The camel spider isn't a true spider—it's a different type of arachnid, and it eats scorpions, spiders, and mice.

Hamadryas baboon

These monkeys live in troops of up to 1,000. They spend nights on ledges of cliffs, but come down to the ground each day to find food.

Rock hyrax

Although it looks more like a guinea pig, the plant-eating rock hyrax is related to the elephant. It even grows two tiny tusks!

Indian forests

India's forests can be wet or dry, but all are warm and tropical. Many trees have broad leaves that they lose in the dry season. For animals, the forests provide food and shelter. However, since trees are cut down for wood or to make farmland, animals like the Bengal tiger have fewer places to live.

Location

Indian forests stretch from the Himalayan mountains south to the Indian Ocean. The weather here is hot or warm most of the year.

PAKISTAN

THAR DESERT

INDIA

Ganges

Yamuna

New Delhi

Ganges

Narmada

Godavari

Krishna

ARABIAN SEA

BAY OF BENGAL

Andaman and Nicobar islands

SRI LANKA

Colombo

Sri Jayawardenepura Kotte

N W E S

Bengal tiger
This tiger's canine teeth (fangs) grow up to 4 in (10 cm) long.

Peafowl
Male peafowl are called peacocks. They use their bright, eyespotted feathers to attract mates.

Indian grey mongoose
Mongooses kill scorpions by throwing them against a hard surface until they crack.

Indian cobra
The cobra hunts lizards, rodents, and frogs. Venom from its bite stops its prey from being able to move.

Indian rhinoceros
The Indian rhino's horn grows to 2 ft (60 cm) long. It's made from keratin—just like our hair.

Indian giant squirrel
The giant squirrel builds nests in trees that are the same size as eagles' nests.

Asian elephant
Asia's largest land mammal is much smaller than its African cousin. It spends three-quarters of its day eating plants.

The Indian giant hornet's bright orange color makes it easy to spot.

Indian giant hornet

The giant hornet is the world's largest—and probably angriest—wasp. It grows up to 2 in (5 cm) long and will sting anything that even slightly disturbs its nest.

Sloth bear

The shy sloth bear digs ants and termites with its long, curved claws. As it laps them up, its loud slurping can be heard from several miles away.

SCALE

0 200 miles

0 200 kilometers

HABITAT KEY

- Wetlands
- Mountains
- Cold desert
- Coniferous forests
- Deciduous forests
- Tropical forests

Female orchid mantises look like flowers. Males are smaller and duller in color.

Orchid mantis

This insect disguises itself as a pink-and-white orchid flower. When other insects land nearby, they are caught unaware as the mantis strikes.

Bornean orangutan

Fruit-eating orangutans live in trees. They bend branches into nests to sleep in at night. Orangutans live alone, unlike other great apes.

Southeast Asian rain forest

The Southeast Asian rain forests are some of the oldest on Earth, and they are home to hundreds of animal species. As the rain forests are cut down, however, amazing animals like the Sumatran rhinoceros become rarer and rarer.

INDIA
CHINA
MYANMAR
VIETNAM
LAOS
CAMBODIA
THAILAND
MALAYSIA
Hainan
ANDAMAN SEA
Andaman Islands
Nicobar Islands
GULF OF THAILAND
Sumatra
Borneo
Java
INDIAN OCEAN
Hanoi
Nay Pyi Daw
Vientiane
Bangkok
Phnom Penh
Putrajaya
Kuala Lumpur
SINGAPORE
Jakarta

Lar gibbon

Gibbons sing in the treetops every morning to tell other gibbons where their territory is.

Purple sunbird

Adult sunbirds drink nectar with their long, curved bills. They feed their chicks insects.

Large flying fox

Its foxlike face gives this large fruit bat its name.

Water buffalo

The domesticated water buffalo is widely used to plough paddy (rice) fields.

Wallace's flying frog

This frog jumps from tree to tree, using its webbed feet and loose skin like a parachute.

Common flying dragon

Special skin stretched over extra-long ribs lets this lizard glide through the rain forest.

Sumatran rhinoceros

This rare, endangered rain-forest rhino has two horns.

Rafflesia flower

This is the biggest single flower in the world. It smells like rotting flesh!

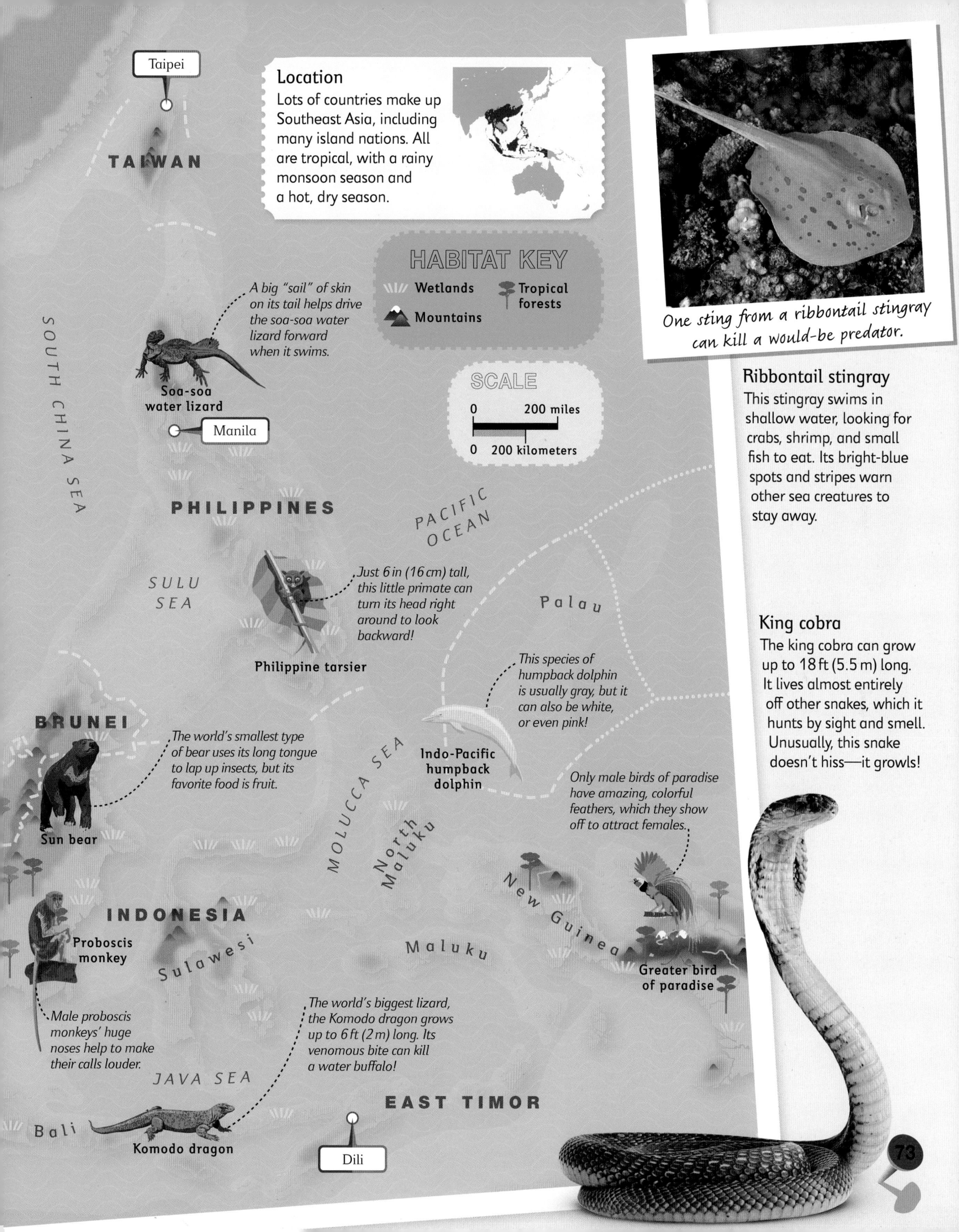

One sting from a ribbontail stingray can kill a would-be predator.

Ribbontail stingray

This stingray swims in shallow water, looking for crabs, shrimp, and small fish to eat. Its bright-blue spots and stripes warn other sea creatures to stay away.

King cobra

The king cobra can grow up to 18 ft (5.5 m) long. It lives almost entirely off other snakes, which it hunts by sight and smell. Unusually, this snake doesn't hiss—it growls!

Gobi desert

The Gobi is Asia's largest desert. It spans more than 460,000 sq miles (1.2 million sq km). Temperatures here can be as scorching hot as 122° F (50° C) and as freezing cold as -40° F (-40° C), but many tough animal species are able to survive despite the extreme conditions.

Gobi bear This is the Earth's rarest bear. Fewer than 50 Gobi bears remain in the desert, their only home.

Mongolian wild ass The wild ass waits for rare rain showers. After the showers, it can feed on fresh grass.

Mongolian marmot This rodent spends winters in its burrow, where it is safe from predators such as eagles.

Long-eared jerboa This tiny, mouselike jerboa hops around the desert at night, looking for tasty insects to eat.

This jerboa's enormous ears are almost as long as its body! Scientists think they release heat, keeping the jerboa cool.

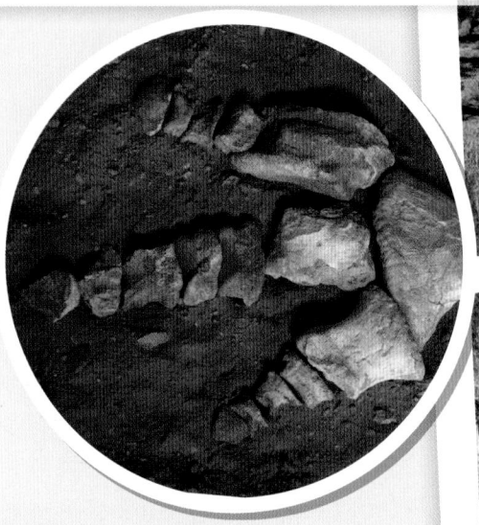

Dinosaur fossil

The Gobi tells us a lot about prehistoric wildlife. Hundreds of dinosaur fossils of many types have been found here—including some from 250 million years ago! This was also first place in the world where dinosaur eggs were identified.

Marbled polecats are named after the pattern on their backs.

Marbled polecat

This little predator doesn't see very well, but it has no trouble finding most of its prey by smell. It hunts rodents, birds, and reptiles—mostly during cool desert nights.

Great bustard Each year, male great bustards grow "whiskers" that look a lot like ears of wheat!
The great bustard flies with slow, steady beats of its wings, which end in long, white feathers.
Yarkand gazelle Unlike other gazelles, the Yarkland doesn't "bound." If scared, it sprints away as fast as it can!
Przewalski's wild horse This wild horse is always on the move, looking for water and short grasses to eat.
Bactrian camel
The Bactrian camel has two humps, where it stores fat to help it survive for long periods without food. If it can't find enough plants to eat, it will eat bones, rope, or even a tent!
Location
The Gobi stretches across northwestern China and southern Mongolia. The average rainfall here is less than 8 in (190 mm) a year!
Saxaul tree
The gnarly saxaul has a lot of roots to anchor it in the sand. Its tiny leaves keep it from losing too much moisture, and it stores water in its bark. If you press a few pieces together, water comes out!

Australasia

Australia, New Zealand, Papua New Guinea, and thousands of small islands make up the Australasia region. From deserts, mountains, and rain forests to beaches and coral reefs, the habitats here are home to many animals only found in this part of the world.

Australian coast

The western Australian coast is home to hundreds of fish, mammals, and bird species. Australian pelicans often land here to enjoy the sand and sun after staying in the air for 24 hours!

Northern Mariana Islands **(UNITED STATES)**

PHILIPPINE SEA

Guam **(UNITED STATES)**

MICRONESIA

PALAU

PAPUA NEW GUINEA

ARAFURA SEA

TIMOR SEA

Christmas Island **(AUSTRALIA)**

Ashmore and Cartier Islands **(AUSTRALIA)**

Coral Sea Islands **(AUSTRALIA)**

CORAL SEA

Cocos (Keeling) Islands **(AUSTRALIA)**

INDIAN OCEAN

Northern Territory

Queensland

AUSTRALIA

Western Australia

South Australia

New South Wales

Victoria

Tasmania

N W E S

Macquarie Island **(AUSTRALIA)**

Australian outback

The hot, dry center of Australia is known as the outback, or the "bush." Because it is mostly desert, very few people live here, but some amazing animals have found ways to survive the tough desert conditions.

Snares Islands

This New Zealand island group, north of the Auckland Islands, is protected from humans so native animal species can thrive. One is the Snares penguin, which nests only on these islands—on the ground, under trees and shrubs.

New Guinea forests

Forests cover two-thirds of the island of Papua New Guinea. Around 760 bird species and 25,000 plant species live here, as does the Goodfellow's tree kangaroo, which climbs trees to eat leaves.

Coral reefs

Coral reefs, like this one in French Polynesia, make up about one percent of the ocean floor—but they are home to almost a quarter of all ocean species. Lots of fish, such as these gold-lined sea breams, gather in the reefs to eat.

Australia

Australia is the world's largest island. Most of it is made of hot, dry desert called "the outback." In the hottest months, some of Australia's lakes may dry up completely. However, there are rain forests here, too, and many of the animals that live in Australia are found nowhere else.

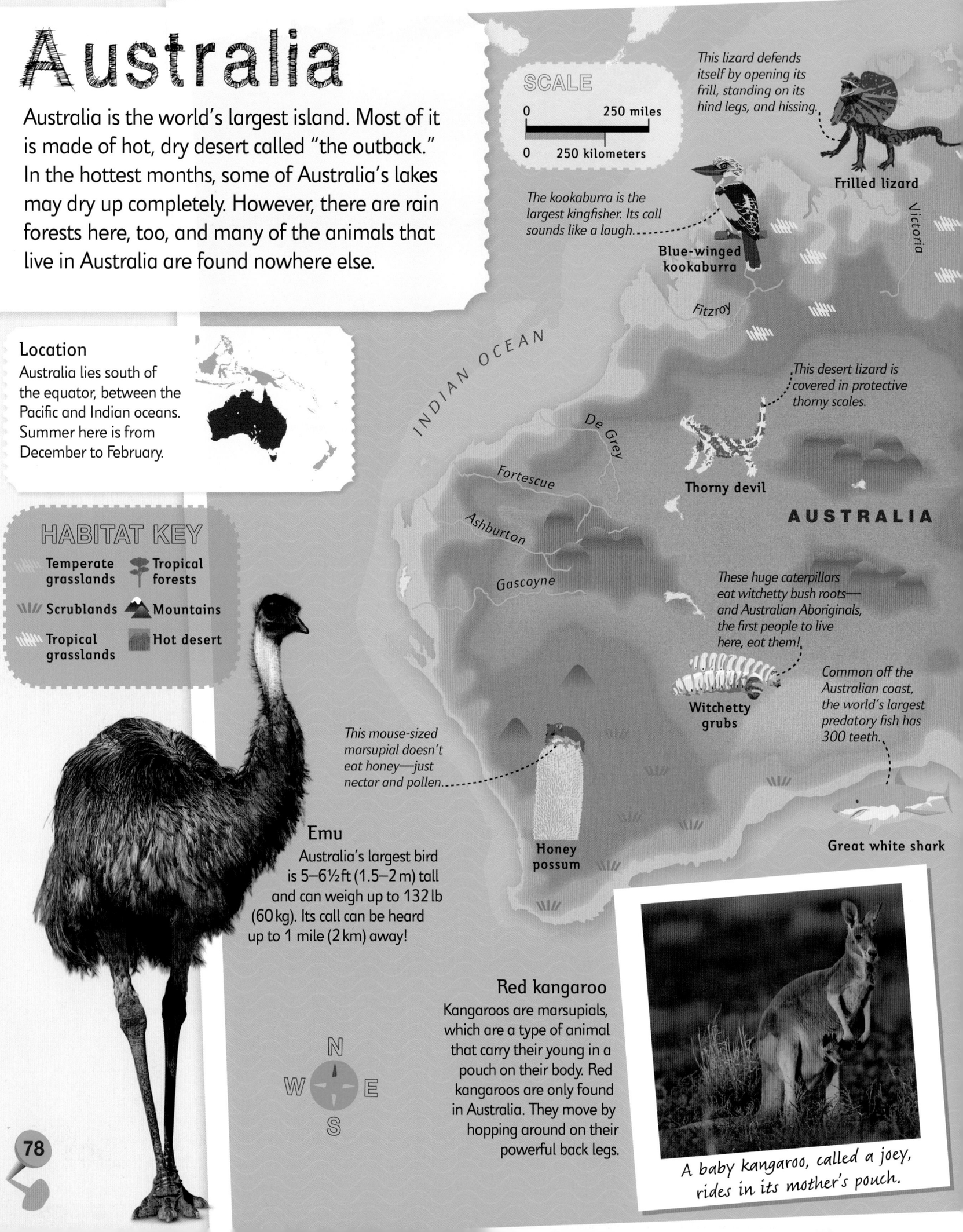

Location

Australia lies south of the equator, between the Pacific and Indian oceans. Summer here is from December to February.

HABITAT KEY

- Temperate grasslands
- Tropical forests
- Scrublands
- Mountains
- Tropical grasslands
- Hot desert

Emu

Australia's largest bird is 5–6½ ft (1.5–2 m) tall and can weigh up to 132 lb (60 kg). Its call can be heard up to 1 mile (2 km) away!

Red kangaroo

Kangaroos are marsupials, which are a type of animal that carry their young in a pouch on their body. Red kangaroos are only found in Australia. They move by hopping around on their powerful back legs.

A baby kangaroo, called a joey, rides in its mother's pouch.

PAPUA NEW GUINEA
Redbacks are one of the most venomous of Australia's 10,000 spider species.
Earth's largest reptile is also found in India and Southeast Asia.
Redback spider
Mitchell
GREAT BARRIER REEF
Saltwater crocodile
Flinders
This dangerous snake is responsible for the most deaths by snakebite in Australia. Watch out!
Eastern brown snake
A webbed membrane allows this tiny mammal to glide more than 151 ft (46 m) between trees.
Sugar glider
This intelligent wild dog rarely barks, but it loves to howl.
This plant-eating burrower is a marsupial, but its pouch points backward. Also, its poop is cube shaped!
Dingo
Darling
Common wombat
BLUE MOUNTAINS
Platypus
Murray
Canberra
This egg-laying mammal has webbed feet and a ducklike bill.
TASMAN SEA
GREAT AUSTRALIAN BIGHT
This animal is the size of a small dog. It's called a devil because it is so aggressive.
Tasmanian devil
The short-beaked echidna's sharp spines repel predators.
Short-beaked echidna
Also called the spiny anteater, this strange-looking mammal lays eggs. It uses its long, sticky tongue to eat grubs, termites, and ants.
Koala
Often mistakenly called bears, koalas are marsupials. Once big enough to leave the pouch, baby koalas ride on the parents' backs. Koalas mostly eat eucalyptus (gum tree) leaves, such as those found in southeastern Australia.

Auckland tree wetas can raise their spiny back legs for defense.

Auckland tree weta

Wetas are much larger cousins of crickets. A tree weta's body is about 1½ in (4 cm) long, but a giant weta can be 4 in (10 cm)—longer than your hand!

New Zealand

New Zealand is made up of two main islands—North and South Island—and many smaller ones. Lots of birds live here, some of which cannot fly. Unfortunately, many were killed by cats, rats, and other predators brought by European settlers. Now, rare birds such as the kakapo are protected.

These huge trees only grow on the North Island. Birds eat the seeds from the cones they produce.

Kauri

This bus-sized whale often raises its tail like a sail, letting the wind push it along the surface of the ocean.

Southern right whale

New Zealand's national symbol, the kiwi is a bird that cannot fly. It lives mostly in burrows and only comes out at night.

North Island brown kiwi

Bats are New Zealand's only native mammals. This one spends more time on the ground than in the air.

New Zealand lesser short-tailed bat

BAY OF PLENTY

Waikato

North Island

Lake Taupo

Hawke Bay

TASMAN SEA

N W E S

SCALE

0 250 miles

0 250 kilometers

New Zealand land snail

This enormous snail grows to 3½ in (9 cm) across and loves to eat earthworms.

This rare frog lives mostly on tiny Stephens Island, where it is safe from tuataras and rats.

Hamilton's frog

Wellington

Location

Located in the southwestern Pacific Ocean, New Zealand's closest neighbor is Australia, 932 miles (1,500 km) to the northwest.

HABITAT KEY
Temperate Grasslands
Deciduous forests
Mountains
Found only in New Zealand, this crayfish buries itself in mud to survive droughts.
Northern koura
Hector's dolphin
Highly endangered, this social little dolphin only grows up to 4½ ft (1.4 m) long.
New Zealand pigeon
Also called the kereru, this blue-green bird eats mostly fruit. It has a red bill, eyes, and feet.
TASMAN SEA
SOUTHERN ALPS
Lake Tekapo
Lake Pukaki
Lake Ohau
Lake Hawea
Lake Wanaka
South Island
The yellow-eyed penguin lays its eggs in forests, and hunts for food up to 15 miles (24 km) away.
Yellow-eyed penguin
The blue damselfly can turn itself darker to get more warmth from the sun.
Blue damselfly
Lake Te Anau
This sea lion rests on southern beaches and offshore islands when it isn't hunting squid.
New Zealand sea lion
Clutha
PACIFIC OCEAN
So rare they are almost extinct, these large, flightless parrots live only in New Zealand.
Kakapo
Stewart Island
Its large eyes help the nocturnal morepork to see at night.
Morepork
This small, dark owl got its name because its call sounds like "more pork"! It sleeps in forests during the day. At night it hunts insects, such as the weta.
Kea
Scientists think this cat-sized parrot is as smart as a four-year-old child. It lives on the South Island and makes a laughlike squeal.
Tuatara
This reptile's closest relatives were around at the time of the dinosaurs. Tuataras like cool weather and can live for up to 100 years!

Great Barrier Reef

The world's largest chain of coral reefs, the Great Barrier Reef lies just off Australia's northeastern coast. It's so big that it can be seen from space, and it is home to more than 1,500 types of fish.

Dugongs can live for 70 years or more in the wild.

Dugong

This slow-moving mammal eats nothing but plants. It pulls seagrass out by the roots with its flexible upper lip. Dugongs are also called "sea cows," because they graze like cows.

Coral

Living corals are made up of tiny animals called coral polyps that catch bits of food with their tentacles. The polyps make hard cases from minerals to protect themselves, and these build up over many years into a reef.

Regal tang Also called surgeonfish, tangs have a scalpel-like spine at the base of their tail on both sides.

Giant barrel sponge The barrel sponge is an animal that grows up to 6 ft (1.8 m) across—and it has no brain!

Sea slug Sea slugs eat corals, sea anemones, sponges, and fish eggs. Their bright colors warn predators away.

Blue starfish Tiny suckers, called tube feet, cover the underside of starfish and let them crawl over the reef.

The reef has many different types of coral. In addition to hard corals, which build the reef, there are also soft corals.

Starfish can regrow a damaged or lost arm. Some can even grow a whole new starfish from just part of an arm.

Blubber jellyfish Each of this creature's eight stumpy arms has several mouths that move food to the animal's stomach.

Potato cod The potato cod hunts fish, crabs, and crayfish. It's so curious that it can annoy divers.

Blacktip reef shark This medium-sized shark loves the shallows. It can swim in water just 12 in (30 cm) deep.

Green sea turtle Green sea turtles are black when they hatch. They change color over the next 25 to 50 years.

Olive sea snake This snake breathes air, and it has a large lung that lets it swim for hours between breaths.

Orange clown fish Clown fish have coats of slime that let them live in sea anemones without being stung.

The peacock mantis shrimp has the fastest punch in the animal world.

Peacock mantis shrimp

Only 1–7 in (3–18 cm) long, this shrimp is deadly. Its clublike arms can punch hard enough to break the shells of crabs—and even aquarium glass!

Location

The Great Barrier Reef runs for 1,429 miles (2,300 km) off the coast of the state of Queensland, Australia.

Giant clam

This clam is so big, it can no longer move. It lives attached to the reef, where it sucks in plankton to eat with a tubelike organ called a siphon.

Most sea creatures avoid sea anemones because they sting, but clown fish live among their tentacles for protection. In return, they bring the anemones food.

Antarctica

The world's coldest continent, Antarctica is also its most remote, meaning it is far from any other land mass. Ice more than 1 mile (1.6 km) thick covers most of it, and temperatures go down to -129°F (-89.2°C), too extreme for many animals. Since it doesn't rain here, Antarctica is considered a desert.

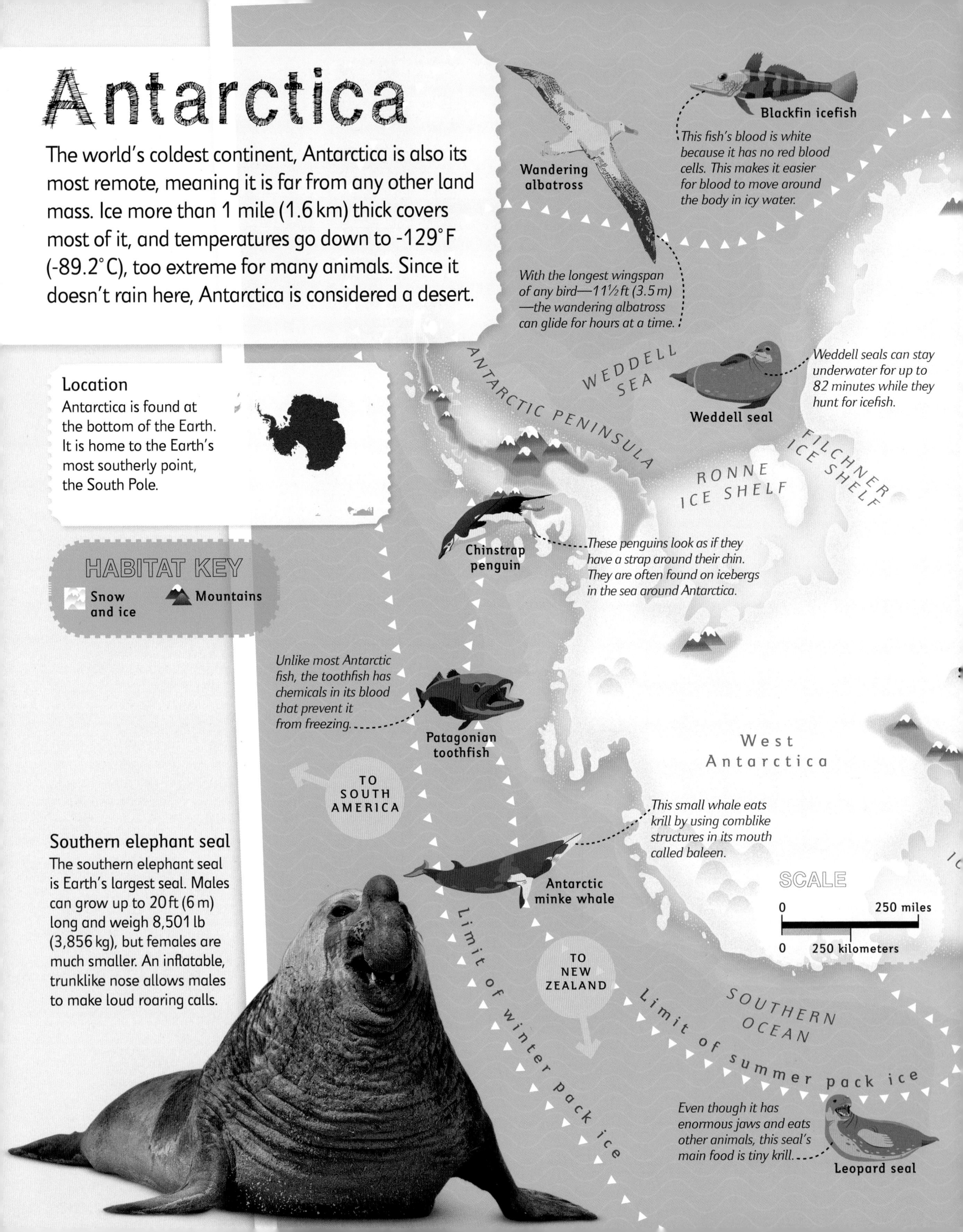

Location

Antarctica is found at the bottom of the Earth. It is home to the Earth's most southerly point, the South Pole.

HABITAT KEY

Snow and ice

Mountains

Southern elephant seal

The southern elephant seal is Earth's largest seal. Males can grow up to 20 ft (6 m) long and weigh 8,501 lb (3,856 kg), but females are much smaller. An inflatable, trunklike nose allows males to make loud roaring calls.

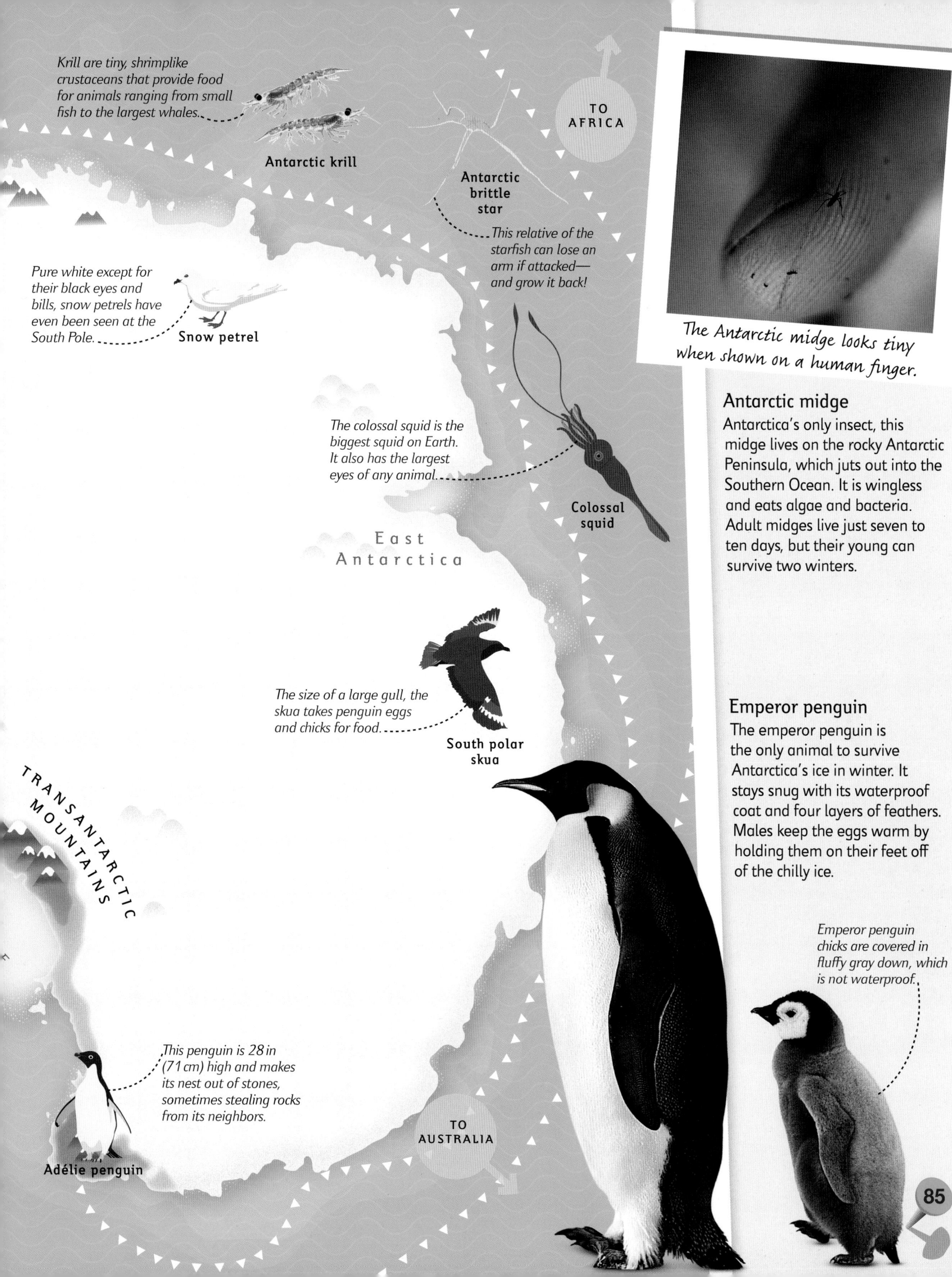

The Antarctic midge looks tiny when shown on a human finger.

Antarctic midge

Antarctica's only insect, this midge lives on the rocky Antarctic Peninsula, which juts out into the Southern Ocean. It is wingless and eats algae and bacteria. Adult midges live just seven to ten days, but their young can survive two winters.

Emperor penguin

The emperor penguin is the only animal to survive Antarctica's ice in winter. It stays snug with its waterproof coat and four layers of feathers. Males keep the eggs warm by holding them on their feet off of the chilly ice.

The Arctic

The Arctic is the Earth's northernmost region. Animals here must survive freezing temperatures. Ice and snow cover the area in winter, and the water of the Arctic Ocean freezes over. In summer, much of the ice melts, revealing a treeless habitat on the surrounding land called tundra.

A polar bear's white fur helps it blend in with its habitat.

Polar bear

The polar bear actually has black skin, but it is covered by thick fur to keep the bear warm. A strong swimmer, the polar bear hunts seals, which it can smell from 1 mile (1.6 km) away.

SCALE

0 250 miles

0 250 kilometers

HABITAT KEY

Mountains

Coniferous forests

Snow and ice

USA

CANADA

RUSSIA

CHUKCHI SEA

EAST SIBERIAN SEA

BEAUFORT SEA

ARCTIC OCEAN

LAPTEV SEA

Lichen is one of the few things reindeer find to eat during Arctic winters.

Reindeer lichen

Reindeer

Both male and female reindeer have antlers. They use their hooves to dig for food under the snow.

Arctic tern

This bird flies 24,900 miles (40,000 km) from the Arctic to the Antarctic each year to follow warmer weather.

Musk ox

Hunted by wolves and sometimes polar bears, musk oxen form a circle when threatened.

This cod has substances in its blood that prevent it from freezing in the polar cold.

Arctic cod

Lemmings are small rodents that live on the tundra, eating grass, seeds, and moss.

Siberian brown lemming

Its pure-white coat makes this hare almost invisible in the snow.

Arctic hare

North Pole

Beluga

Born gray, beluga whales don't turn white until they are as old as eight years.

This whale's spiral tusk is actually a tooth that grows up to 10 ft (3 m) long.

Narwhal

KARA SEA

A very slow swimmer, this shark cruises deep in the ocean, feeding on carrion (dead animals).

Greenland shark

In winter, this fox turns white to help it hide in the snow as it hunts for Arctic hares.

Arctic fox

Walrus

BARENTS SEA

A thick layer of blubber (fat) keeps walruses warm when they hunt for food in icy waters.

GREENLAND (DENMARK)

GREENLAND SEA

Lemmings are one of the snowy owl's main sources of food. It can eat five lemmings in a day.

ARCTIC CIRCLE

Snowy owl

NORWAY

FINLAND

SWEDEN

Location

The Arctic includes the extreme northern parts of Europe, Asia, and North America. Winters get as cold as -90°F (-68°C).

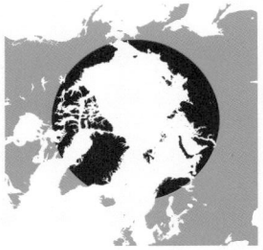

Harp seal

These seals are named for the pattern on their backs, which looks like the musical instrument. Harp seals are born white, but turn dark after three weeks.

An adult harp seal watches its white-furred cub.

Arctic fox

In summer, the Arctic fox sheds its white coat, turning gray-brown so it blends in with its surroundings.

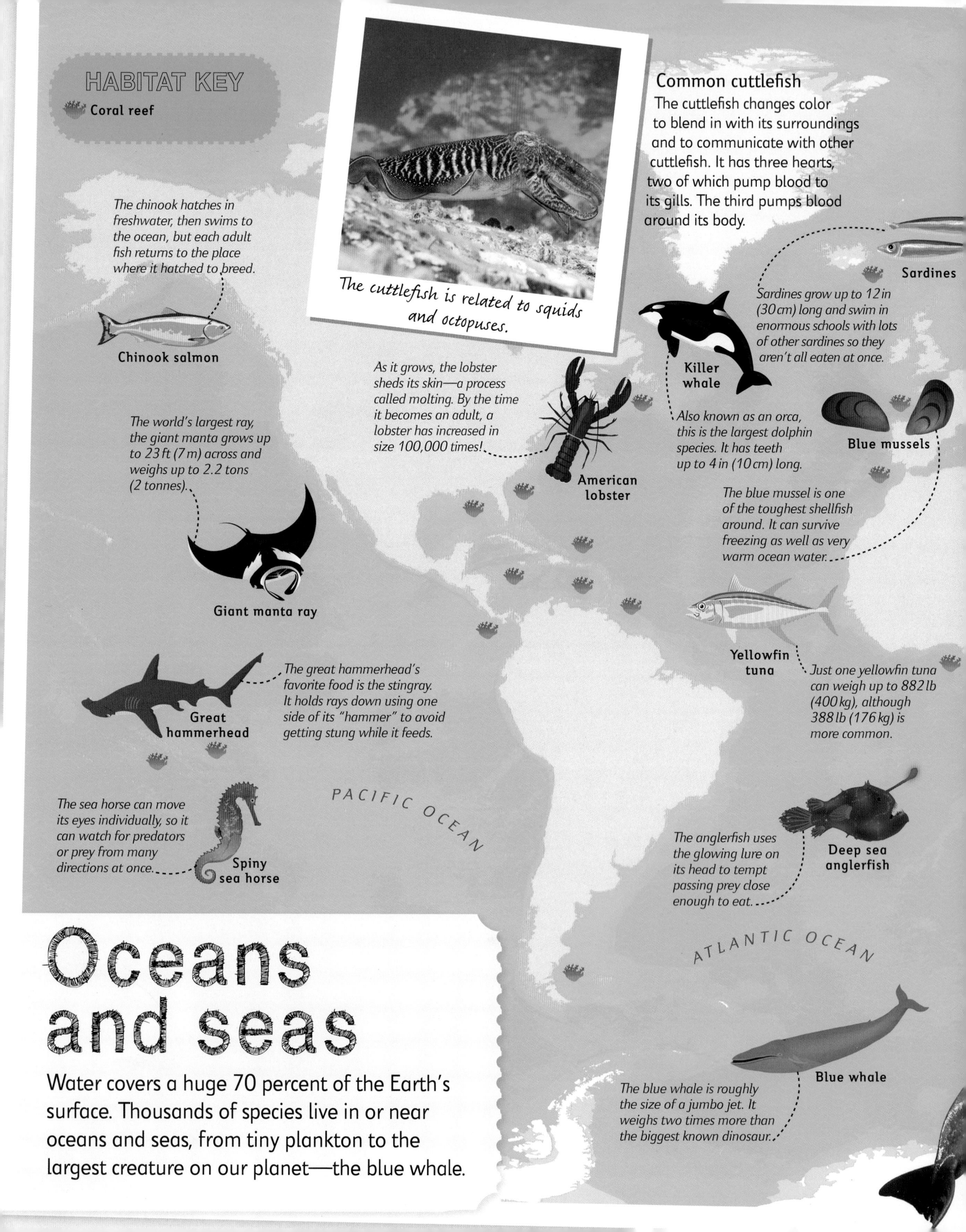

Oceans and seas

Water covers a huge 70 percent of the Earth's surface. Thousands of species live in or near oceans and seas, from tiny plankton to the largest creature on our planet—the blue whale.

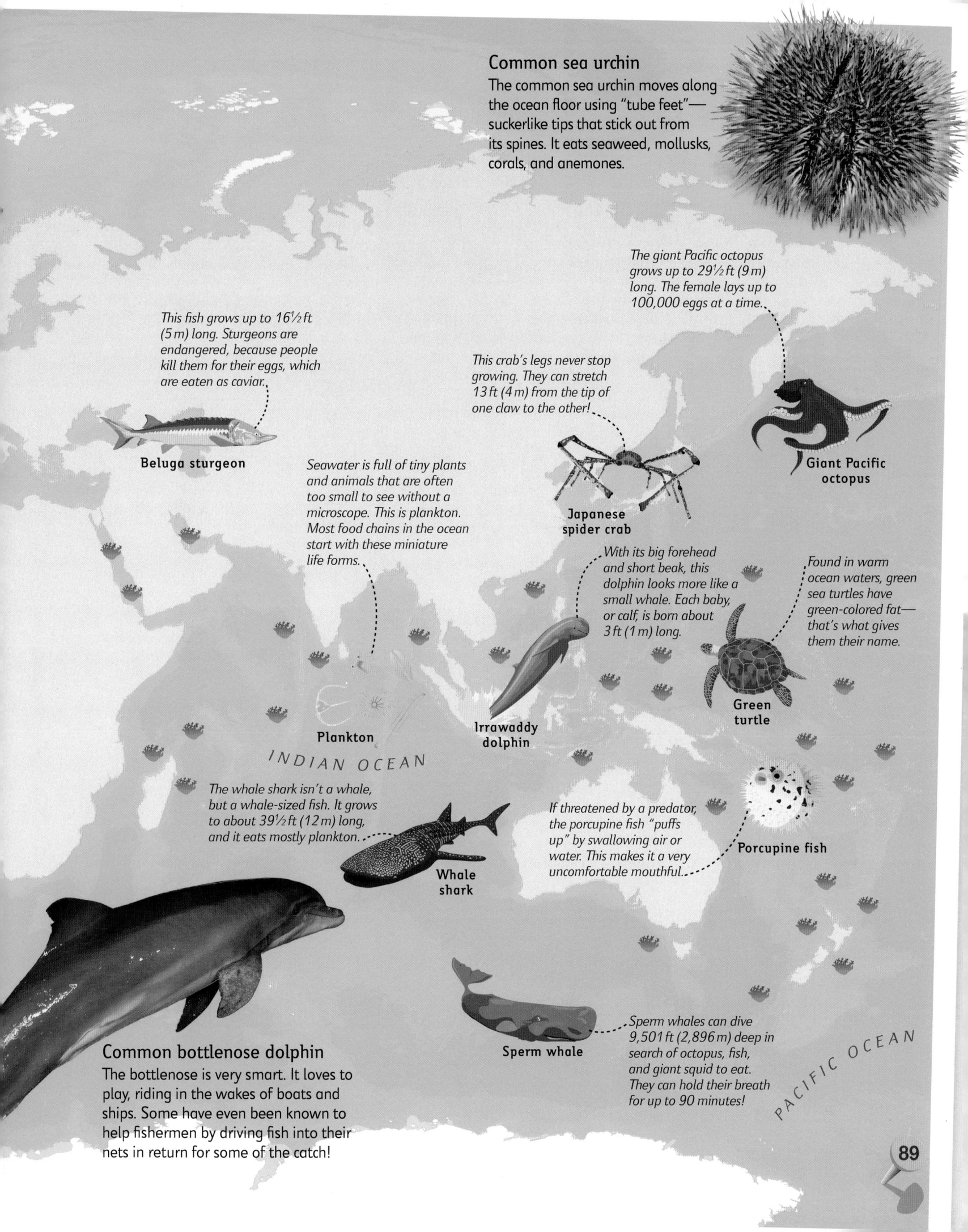
Common sea urchin
The common sea urchin moves along the ocean floor using "tube feet"—suckerlike tips that stick out from its spines. It eats seaweed, mollusks, corals, and anemones.
The giant Pacific octopus grows up to 29½ ft (9 m) long. The female lays up to 100,000 eggs at a time.
This fish grows up to 16½ ft (5 m) long. Sturgeons are endangered, because people kill them for their eggs, which are eaten as caviar.
Beluga sturgeon
This crab's legs never stop growing. They can stretch 13 ft (4 m) from the tip of one claw to the other!
Giant Pacific octopus
Japanese spider crab
Seawater is full of tiny plants and animals that are often too small to see without a microscope. This is plankton. Most food chains in the ocean start with these miniature life forms.
With its big forehead and short beak, this dolphin looks more like a small whale. Each baby, or calf, is born about 3 ft (1 m) long.
Found in warm ocean waters, green sea turtles have green-colored fat—that's what gives them their name.
Green turtle
Irrawaddy dolphin
Plankton
INDIAN OCEAN
The whale shark isn't a whale, but a whale-sized fish. It grows to about 39½ ft (12 m) long, and it eats mostly plankton.
If threatened by a predator, the porcupine fish "puffs up" by swallowing air or water. This makes it a very uncomfortable mouthful.
Porcupine fish
Whale shark
Common bottlenose dolphin
The bottlenose is very smart. It loves to play, riding in the wakes of boats and ships. Some have even been known to help fishermen by driving fish into their nets in return for some of the catch!
Sperm whale
Sperm whales can dive 9,501 ft (2,896 m) deep in search of octopus, fish, and giant squid to eat. They can hold their breath for up to 90 minutes!
PACIFIC OCEAN

ATLAS PICTURE QUIZ

This area in northern Africa is the largest hot desert in the world.

This area of scrubland shares its name with the sea it borders.

This high prairie stretches across parts of Canada and the United States.

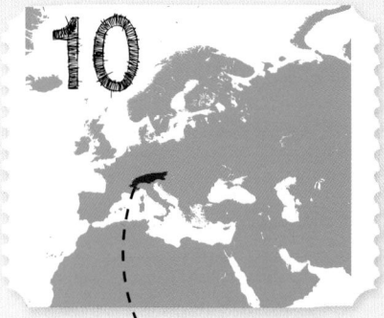

This famous mountain range in Europe includes lakes, glaciers, meadows, and forests.

NAME THE HABITAT

Here are some of the habitats and islands that appear in this atlas. Can you name them? Look at the clues to help you. The answers are on page 91.

This country is made of two main islands and lots of other, smaller ones.

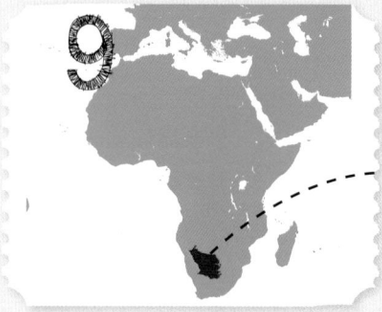

This desert in southern Africa gets enough rain for grass and other plants to grow.

This South American rain forest is home to 2.5 million different species of insects.

These volcanic islands are home to many unique animals named after the area.

The rain forests of this area are some of the oldest on Earth.

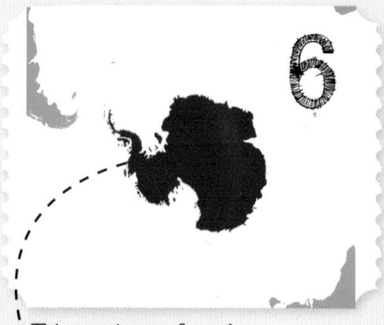

This continent, found at the bottom of the Earth, is the world's coldest.

Answers: Page 90 Name the habitat: 1. Sahara desert (pages 36–37), 2. Kalahari (page 42), 3. Great Plains (page 12), 4. New Zealand (pages 80–81), 5. Amazon rain forest (pages 22–23), 6. Antarctica (pages 84–85), 7. Southeast Asia (pages 72–73), 8. The Galápagos (page 29), 9. Mediterranean scrubland (pages 56–57), 10. The Alps (page 54).
Page 91 Guess the icon: 1. Clouded leopard (page 68), 2. Colossal squid (page 85), 3. 50,000 (page 42), 4. Green (page 56), 5. One year (page 51), 6. The Andes (page 24), 7. 29½ in or 75 cm (page 56), 8. Common wombat (page 79), 9. Western deserts (page 14), 10. African spurred tortoise (page 37), 11. Congo Basin (page 38), 12. Giant ameiva (page 31), 13. Resplendent quetzal (page 16), 14. Narwhal (page 87), 15. Madagascar (page 43), 16. Great bustard (page 55), 17. Goliath birdeater (page 23), 18. Yellow-eyed penguin (page 81), 19. Monarch butterfly (page 11), 20. Vampire bat (page 17), 21. 4 in or 10 cm (page 71), 22. Wallace's flying frog (page 72), 23. Stag beetle (page 52).

Glossary

amphibians
Cold-blooded animals that live both on land and in water, such as frogs and newts

birds
Warm-blooded animals that are covered in feathers and have a bill, many of which can fly, such as eagles

climate
Normal weather pattern during the year in any part of the world

coniferous tree
Type of tree with cones and needlelike leaves that keeps its leaves all year round

continents
Seven large areas of land that the world is divided into: Africa, Antarctica, Asia, Australasia, Europe, North America, and South America

coral reefs
Rocklike structures formed by coral animals in the shallow waters along coasts

deciduous tree
Type of tree that loses its leaves in the fall or the dry season

desert
Dry region that gets very little rainfall in a year. Deserts can be hot or cold

endangered
Word used to describe a species of plant or animal with only a few living members left

equator
Imaginary line around the middle of the Earth

extinct
Word used to describe a plant or animal species that has no living members

fish
Cold-blooded animals that live in water and have gills and fins, such as salmon

habitat
Environment in which an animal or plant lives

hibernation
Sleeplike state some animals enter in winter

invertebrates
Cold-blooded animals without a backbone, such as insects, spiders, or squids

island
Piece of land that has water all around it

mammals
Warm-blooded animals that have hair and feed their young with milk, such as mice

mangroves
Trees that live in salty water and have long, stiltlike roots

marsupial
Type of mammal that keeps its young in a pouch

migration
Movement of a large number of animals from one area to another. Animals migrate to follow warmer weather and to find food

mountain
Area of land that rises up much higher than the land around it to form a peak

national park
Area of countryside that has been preserved in its natural state by the government of a country to protect the wildlife there and for people to enjoy

native
Word used to describe an animal that comes from a particular area or country

nocturnal
Word used to describe animals that are awake during the night

ocean
Very large sea. There are five oceans: the Pacific, Atlantic, Indian, Arctic, and Southern

plain
Area of flat land with few trees, often covered with grass

plateau
Large area of high, flat land

polar regions
Areas within the polar circles. Polar regions are covered in snow and ice for most of the year and are extremely cold

predator
Animal that hunts other living animals for food

prey
Animal that is hunted for food

rain forests
Dense forests with very high rainfall. Most are near the equator and are also very hot

reptiles
Cold-blooded animals covered in dry, scaly skin such as snakes, tortoises, and crocodiles

scrubland
Area of land covered in different types of grass, and small trees and bushes

species
Particular group of animals or plants that share similar features

taiga
Area of cold, coniferous forest found near the Arctic Circle

temperate grassland
Large areas of grass found in regions with hot and cold seasons, such as prairie, steppe, and pampas

temperate regions
Areas with hot and cold seasons found between tropical and polar regions

tropical grassland
Large areas of grass found in areas that are hot all year round, such as savanna and cerrado

tropical regions
Areas that are hot all year round, found near the equator between the Tropic of Cancer and the Tropic of Capricorn

tundra
Cold, treeless plains found near the Arctic Circle

wetlands
Land with wet, spongy soil, such as a marsh or swamp

Index

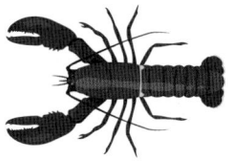

A

aardvarks 42, 44
acacia trees 34, 41
Afghanistan 60, 64, 65
Africa 34–45
Alaska 10
Albania 47, 52, 57
albatrosses 84
Algeria 34, 36
alligators 18
The Alps 54
Amazon rain forest 20, 22–23
Amazon River 21
Andes 21, 24–25, 32–33
Andorra 46
anglerfish 88
Angola 34–35, 40, 42
anhingas 18
Antarctic Circle 6
Antarctica 84–85
anteaters 22, 30
antelopes 12, 36, 37, 41, 42, 45, 62, 65, 67, 69, 70, 75
ants 23, 30, 52
Arabian Peninsula 60, 70
Arctic 86–87
Arctic Circle 6
Argentina 20, 25, 26–27
armadillos 15, 31
Armenia 60, 65
Asia 60–75
Asian steppe 64
assassin bugs 26
asses 67, 74
Atlantic Ocean 88
Australasia 76–83
Australia 76, 78–79, 82–83
Austria 46, 52, 54
aye-ayes 43
Azerbaijan 60, 65

B

baboons 40, 70
badgers 10, 50, 59
Bahamas 9, 17
Bahrain 60, 70
Bangladesh 61, 67
baobabs 43
barracudas 18
barrier islands 9
batfish 17
bats 17, 48, 53, 59, 72, 80
bears 8, 10, 13, 24, 33, 47, 62, 66, 71, 73, 86
beavers 11, 59
bee-eaters 39
bees 51
beetles 22, 41, 52
Belarus 47, 48, 53, 55, 58–59
Belgium 46, 52
Belize 9, 16
Benin 34
bharals 67
Bhutan 61, 67
Białowieża Forest 58–59
birch trees 62
birds of paradise 73
bison 8, 12, 59
blue tits 52
bobcats 14
Bolivia 20, 23, 24, 28, 30
bongos 38
bonobos 38
boobies 29
Borneo 61, 72
Bosnia & Herzegovina 47, 52, 57
Botswana 40, 42
Brazil 20–21, 22–23, 24, 28, 30–31
British Isles 46, 50–51, 52
brittle stars 85
Brunei 61, 73
buffaloes 38, 72
Bulgaria 47, 55, 57
Burkina Faso 34
Burundi 35
bush babies 40
bustards 37, 55, 75
butterflies 11, 22, 54, 68

C

cacti 15
caimans 28
The Camargue 46
Cambodia 61, 72
camels 35, 37, 60, 75
Cameroon 34, 38
Canada 8–9, 10–11, 12–13, 86
Cape Verde 34
capercaillies 49
capybaras 20, 28
caracals 70
caracaras 25, 33
cardinals 13
Caribbean 9, 17
Carpathian Mountains 47
Caspian Sea 64
cats 15, 27, 31, 64, 70
centipedes 56
Central African Republic 34–35, 38
Central America 9, 16
Central Asian deserts 65
Cerrado 30–31
Chad 34–35, 37, 38
chameleons 43, 56
chamois 54
chapis 38
cheetahs 42, 45
cherry trees 69
chickens 12
Chihuahuan desert 15
Chile 20, 25
chimpanzees 39
China 60, 61, 64, 65, 66–67, 68–69, 72, 74–75
chinchillas 25
chipmunks 63
choughs 54
clams 83
climatic zones 6
clown fish 83
coatis 23
cock of the rocks 25
cod 83, 86
colocolos 32
Colombia 20, 22, 24
Comoros 35
condors 25, 32
Congo 34, 38
Congo Basin 38–39
continents 6–7
coral 82
coral reefs 77, 82–83
Cordillera Blanca 32–33
cork oaks 57
cormorants 29
Corsica 56
Costa Rica 9, 16
coyotes 12
coypus 26
crabs 29, 51, 89
cranes 69
crayfish 81
Crete 57
Croatia 46, 52, 54, 57
crocodiles 17, 37, 79
crossbills 49
crows 49
Cuba 9, 17
cuckoos 56
culpeos 33
cuttlefish 88
Cyprus 60
Czech Republic 46, 52

D

damselflies 81
deer 8, 13, 24, 25, 27, 28, 32, 51, 53, 58, 62, 68
Democratic Republic of the Congo 35, 38, 40–41
Denmark 46, 52
desert broom 14
deserts 14–15, 35, 36–37, 42, 60, 65, 70, 74–75, 76, 78, 84
dingoes 79
dinosaur fossils 74
Djibouti 35
dogs 25, 31, 40, 58, 69, 79
dolphins 22, 73, 81, 89
Dominican Republic 9, 17
dormice 51, 53
ducks 33, 49, 68, 69
dugongs 82

E

eagles 8, 12, 23, 39, 45, 49, 55, 64
East Asian forests 68–69
East Timor 61, 73
eastern forests 13
echidnas 79
Ecuador 20, 22, 24
eels 23
Egypt 35, 37
El Salvador 9, 16
elephants 40, 45, 71
emus 78
England 51
equator 6
Equatorial Guinea 34
Eritrea 35, 37
Estonia 47, 48, 52
Ethiopia 35, 37
Europe 46–59
European forests 52–53
European steppe 55
The Everglades 18–19

F

falcons 64
Falkland Islands 21, 25
Fiji 77
Finland 47, 48, 52, 87
fireflies 11
flamingos 21, 24, 41
Florida 18–19
forests 13, 22–23, 35, 52–53, 58–59, 68–69, 71, 77
see also rain forests; taiga
fossas 43
foxes 12, 13, 26, 36, 52, 58, 65, 67, 87
France 46, 52, 54, 56
French Guiana 21, 23
frigate birds 17
frogs 16, 19, 22, 24, 26, 31, 39, 42, 43, 56, 63, 72, 80
fynbos 34

G

Gabon 34, 38
galagos 40
Galápagos 29
gallinules 19
The Gambia 34
gazelles 37, 65, 70, 75
geckos 36, 57
geese 11, 25, 32
geladas 35
Georgia 60
gerbils 65
Germany 46, 52, 54
Ghana 34
gibbons 72
giraffes 34, 41, 44

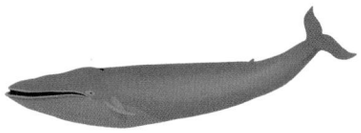
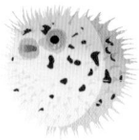

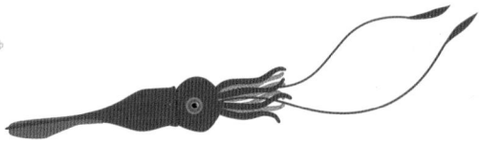

goats 65, 66, 69
Gobi desert 74–75
gorals 69
gorillas 38
grasslands 30–31
see also pampas; savanna; steppes
Great Barrier Reef 82–83
Great Plains 8, 12
Greece 47, 52, 57
Greenland 9, 87
grisons 27
guanacos 32
Guatemala 9, 16
Guinea 34
guinea pigs 24
Guinea-Bissau 34
Guyana 21, 23

H

habitats 5, 6
Haiti 9, 17
hamsters 55
hares 12, 48, 65, 66, 87
hawks 29
heather 46
hedgehogs 50, 65
herons 18
Himalayas 61, 66–67
hippopotamuses 40, 44
hogs 39
Honduras 9, 16
honey badgers 44
hoopoes 53
hornbills 41
hornets 71
horses 46, 60, 64, 70, 75
hummingbirds 15, 16, 33
Hungary 47, 52
hutias 17
hyenas 36
hyraxes 70

I

ibexes 54, 56
icefish 84
Iceland 46, 48
iguanas 29, 30
impalas 41, 45
India 60, 66, 71, 72
Indian forests 71
Indian Ocean 89
Indonesia 61, 73
Iran 65, 70
Iraq 60, 70
Ireland 46, 51
Israel 60, 70
Italy 46, 52, 54, 57
Ivory Coast 34

J

jackals 57
jaguars 23
Jamaica 9, 17
Japan 61, 69
jays 49
jellyfish 83
jerboas 37, 74
Jordan 60, 70

K

kakapos 81
Kalahari desert 42
kangaroos 77, 78
kapok trees 22
kauri trees 80
Kazakhstan 60, 64, 65
keas 81
Kenya 35
kererus 81
kiangs 67
kingfishers 27, 78
Kiribati 77
kites 19, 51
kiwis 80
koalas 79
Komodo dragons 73
kookaburras 78
Kosovo 47, 52, 57
krill 85
Kruger National Park 44–45
Kuwait 60
Kyrgyzstan 60, 64, 65

L

ladybugs 51
Laos 61, 72
Latvia 47, 48, 52
Lebanon 60
lemmings 48, 86, 87
lemurs 43
leopards 38, 61, 67, 68
Lesotho 35
Liberia 34
Libya 34–35, 37
lichen 86
Liechtenstein 46
lions 40, 45
Lithuania 47, 48, 52
lizards 14, 26, 29, 30, 31, 36, 56, 70, 72, 73, 78
llamas 24
locust 36
loons 11
lungfish 39
Luxembourg 46, 52
lynxes 48, 57

M

macaws 9, 30
Macedonia 47, 52, 55, 57
Madagascar 35, 43
magpies 57
Majorca 56
Malawi 35
Malaysia 61, 72
Mali 34, 36
Malta 57
manakins 30
mandrills 38
mantises 72
maras 26
marlins 17
marmots 54, 64, 66, 74
Marshall Islands 77
Mauritania 34, 36
Mauritius 35
meadowlarks 27
Mediterranean scrubland 56–57
Mediterranean Sea 47, 56–57
meerkats 42
Mexico 8–9, 15
mice 51, 53, 55, 59, 66
Micronesia 76
midges 85
millipedes 52
minks 52
Mojave desert 14, 15
Moldova 47, 53
mole rats 55
moles 55
Monaco 46
Mongolia 60, 61, 68, 74–75
mongooses 71
monkeys 16, 23, 28, 41, 56, 68, 69, 70, 73
Montenegro 47, 52, 57
moorland 46
moose 11, 47
Morocco 34, 36
mosquitoes 39
moss 46
moths 43, 57
mountains 8, 24–25, 35, 54, 61, 66–67
Mozambique 35, 41
musk oxen 86
mussels 88
Myanmar (Burma) 61, 67, 72

N

Namibia 34–35, 40, 42
Nauru 77
Nepal 60, 66
Netherlands 46, 52
New Zealand 77, 80–81
newts 55
Nicaragua 9, 16
Niger 34, 37
Nigeria 34, 37
nightingales 55
nightjars 52
North America 8–19
North Korea 61, 69
North Pole 87
Northern Ireland 51
Norway 46, 48, 52, 87

O

oaks 51, 57
oceans 88–89
ocelots 16
octopuses 89
okapis 38
Oman 60, 70
onagers 64
opossums 13, 31
orangutans 61, 72
ospreys 49
ostriches 42
otters 10, 28, 51
outback 76
owls 11, 13, 15, 27, 48, 51, 53, 59, 63, 81, 87

P

Pacific Ocean 88–89
Pakistan 60, 65, 66, 71
Palau 76
pampas 21, 26–27
pampas grass 27
Panama 9, 16
pandas 67
pangolins 39
Pantanal 20, 28
panthers 19
Papua New Guinea 76, 79
Paraguay 21, 23, 28, 30
parrots 38, 81
partridges 70
Patagonia 21
peafowl 71
pelicans 57, 76
penguins 29, 76, 81, 84, 85
Peru 20, 22, 24, 32–33
petrels 85
pheasants 69
Philippines 61, 73
pigeons 53, 81
pigs 17, 39, 56
pine martens 54, 58
piranhas 23
plankton 89
platypuses 79
Poland 47, 52, 58–59
polar bears 86

polar zones 6, 7
polecats 55, 64, 74
ponies 9
porcupine fish 89
porcupines 42
porpoises 51
Portugal 46, 56
possums 78, 79
prairie dogs 8, 12
prairie shoestring 12
ptarmigans 54
Puerto Rico 9, 17
puffins 48
pumas 15

Q

Qatar 60, 70
quetzals 16

R

rabbits 12, 14, 56
raccoons 13, 69
rafflesia flowers 72
rain forest 9, 20, 38–39, 61, 72–73
rats 15
rays 73, 88
Red Sea 35, 37
redwood trees 8
reindeer 86
rheas 21, 26
rhinoceroses 40, 71, 72
roadrunners 15
robins 51, 63
Romania 47, 52, 55, 57
rubythroats 63
Russian Federation 47, 48–49, 53, 55, 60–61, 68–69, 86
Rwanda 35

S

sables 62
Sahara desert 35, 36–37
salamanders 54, 68
salmon 10, 88
salmonberries 10
Samoa 77
San Marino 46
sandgrouse 37
sardines 88
Sardinia 56
Saudi Arabia 60, 70
savanna 34, 40–41, 44, 60
saxaul trees 75
scorpions 37, 38
Scotland 46, 50
scrubland 56–57
sea anemones 83
sea breams 77
sea lions 29, 81
sea urchins 89
seagulls 60
sea horses 88
seals 47, 50, 63, 84, 87
seas 88–89
secretary birds 44
Senegal 34
Serbia 47, 52, 57
seriemas 31
serows 69
serratulas 66
Seychelles 35
sharks 78, 83, 87, 88, 89
sheep 14, 36, 63, 67
shrews 54
shrimps 83
Sicily 57
Sierra Leone 34
skuas 85
skunks 13
sloths 16, 71
Slovakia 47, 52
Slovenia 46, 52, 54
slugs 8, 82
snails 28, 80
snakes 12, 15, 18, 23, 24, 28, 30, 36, 51, 53, 65, 68, 71, 73, 79, 83
Snares Islands 76
solenodons 17
Solomon Islands 77
Somalia 35
Sonoran desert 15
South Africa 34–35, 42, 44–45
South America 20–33
South Korea 61, 69
South Pole 84
South Sudan 35, 38
Southeast Asian rain forest 72–73
Southern savanna 40–41
Spain 46, 56
spiders 14, 19, 23, 79
spiny forest 35
sponges 82
spoonbills 28
spruce trees 49
squid 85
squirrels 13, 50, 59, 62, 64, 71
Sri Lanka 60, 71
starfish 82
starlings 55
steppes 21, 55, 64
stick insects 24
stingrays 73
stoats 49
storks 28
sturgeon 89
Sudan 35, 37
sugar gliders 79
sugar maples 13
sunbirds 72
sunfish 18
Suriname 21
Swaziland 35
Sweden 46, 48, 52, 87
Switzerland 46, 52, 54
Syria 60

T

tahrs 66
taiga 10–11, 47, 48–49, 62–63
Taiwan 61, 73
Tajikistan 60, 64, 65
tamarins 22
tangs 82
Tanzania 35
tapirs 16
tarsiers 73
tayras 16
temperate zones 6, 7
tenrecs 43
termites 31
terns 86
Thailand 61, 72
thorny devils 78
Tibetan Plateau 66–67
tigers 62, 71
toads 49, 58, 67
Togo 34
Tonga 77
toothfish 84
tortoises 14, 29, 37, 43, 57, 64
toucans 23
Trinidad and Tobago 9, 17
trogons 17
Tropic of Cancer 6
Tropic of Capricorn 6
tropical zone 6, 7
tuataras 81
tuna 88
tundra 86
Tunisia 34, 36
turacos 38
Turkey 47, 60
Turkmenistan 60, 65
turtles 10, 17, 18, 83, 89
Tuvalu 77

U

Uganda 35
Ukraine 47, 53, 55
United Arab Emirates 60, 70
United Kingdom 46, 50–51
United States of America (USA) 8–9, 10, 12–15, 18–19, 86
Ural Mountains 49, 55
Uruguay 21, 27
Uzbekistan 60, 64, 65

V

Vanuatu 77
Vatican City 46
Venezuela 17, 20, 22
vicuñas 25
Vietnam 61, 72
vizcachas 27, 32
voles 52
vultures 14, 30, 42, 44, 67

W

Wales 51
walruses 87
warthogs 42
water lilies 28
weasels 53, 67
weavers 42
western deserts 14–15
Western Sahara 34, 36
wetas 80
wetlands 18–19, 20, 28, 46
whales 80, 84, 87, 88, 89
wild boars 47, 53
wildcats 50
wildebeests 41
witchetty grubs 78
wolverines 49
wolves 8, 10, 11, 30, 47, 56, 58, 66
wombats 79
woodpeckers 59, 63
world map 6–7

Y

yaks 61, 66
Yemen 60, 70

Z

Zambia 35, 40–41
zebras 40, 45
Zimbabwe 35, 41

Credits

Dorling Kindersley would like to thank Dr. Don E. Wilson, Curator Emeritus, Department of Vertebrate Zoology, National Museum of Natural History, Smithsonian, for his expert consultation.

The publisher would also like to thank the following people for their help in preparing this book: Kealy Gordon and Ellen Nanney at the Smithsonian; Helen Peters for the index; Polly Goodman for proofreading; Joylon Goddard and Katy Lennon for additional editing; and Jagtar Singh and Sachin Singh for additional design.

Picture Credits:
The publisher would also like to thank the following for their kind permission to reproduce their photographs:

(Key: a-above; b-below/bottom; c-center; f-far; l-left; r-right; t-top)

8 Alamy Stock Photo: John Hyde / Design Pics Inc (c). **iStockphoto.com:** ericfoltz (bl); Pawel Gaul (cl). **9 iStockphoto.com:** John_Wijsman (tr); OGphoto (cr). **11 Alamy Stock Photo:** Danny Green / Nature Picture Library (tl); Vl_K (tr). **Dorling Kindersley:** Jerry Young (br). **12 123RF.com:** wrangel (br). **Corbis:** Ocean (cl). **13 123RF.com:** Marie-Ann Daloia (cr). **Dorling Kindersley:** Jerry Young (tl). **14 Alamy Stock Photo:** Wayne Lynch / All Canada Photos (tc). **SuperStock:** Cyril Ruoso / Minden Pictures (cl). **16 Fotolia:** Eric Isselee (cl). **17 Photolibrary:** Photodisc / Tom Brakefield (tr). **18 Alamy Stock Photo:** WaterFrame_eda (cl). **Dorling Kindersley:** Jerry Young (cr). **Dreamstime.com:** Brian Lasenby (cb). **Getty Images:** Joe McDonald / Corbis Documentary (bl). **18-19 Getty Images:** Tim Graham / Getty Images News. **19 Alamy Stock Photo:** George Grall / National Geographic Creative (bl). **iStockphoto.com:** FernandoAH (tl); madcorona (crb); hakoar (tr); ygluzberg (cl). **20 Alamy Stock Photo:** Denis-Huot Michel / hemis.fr / Hemis (bl). **iStockphoto.com:** Marcelo Horn (cl). 21 123RF.com: belikova (b). **Alamy Stock Photo:** blickwinkel / Wothe (cr). **iStockphoto.com:** Magaiza (tr). **22 iStockphoto.com:** Leonardo Prest Mercon Ro / LeoMercon (cl). **23 123RF.com:** Anan Kaewkhammul (br). **Alamy Stock Photo:** Amazon-Images (cra). **24 SuperStock:** Albert Lleal / Minden Pictures (tc). **25 Dorling Kindersley:** Blackpool Zoo (br). **iStockphoto.com:** webguzs (bl). **26 SuperStock:** Juniors (cl). **27 Alamy Stock Photo:** Johner Images (tr). **Dorling Kindersley:** Gary Ombler (br). **28 123RF.com:** Francisco de Casa Gonzalez (br); Ondřej Prosický (tr). **Alamy Stock Photo:** James Brunker (bl). **29 123RF.com:** mark52 (bl). **Alamy Stock Photo:** Reinhard Dirscherl (cr). **30 Dorling Kindersley:** Greg Dean / Yvonne Dean (cl). **31 naturepl.com:** Luiz Claudio Marigo (br). **SuperStock:** Minden Pictures (cra). **32 123RF.com:** Martin Otero (cl). **Dorling Kindersley:** Hanne Eriksen / Jens Eriksen (fcrb); Prof. Marcio Motta (cb). **Dreamstime.com:** Jeremy Richards (bl). **33 123RF.com:** Martin Schneiter (c). **Dorling Kindersley:** E. J. Peiker (tr). **Dreamstime.com:** Musat Christian (cr). **SuperStock:** Glenn Bartley / All Canada Photos (bl, tl). **34 Alamy Stock Photo:** Michele Burgess (bc); Lars Johansson (cl). **35 Alamy Stock Photo:** Ange (br); Aivar Mikko (tc). **iStockphoto.com:** helovi (cra). **36 Dorling Kindersley:** Jerry Young (br). **38 Dorling Kindersley:** Liberty's Owl, Raptor and Reptile Centre, Hampshire, UK (bl). **39 123RF.com:** Andrey Gudkov (cr); Jatesada Natayo (tr). **41 123RF.com:** pytyczech (bc). **Alamy Stock Photo:** Andrew Mackay (r). **42 Dorling Kindersley:** Wildlife Heritage Foundation, Kent, UK (bl). **Dreamstime.com:** Artushfoto (ftr). **SuperStock:** Alexander Koenders / NiS / Minden Pictures (tr). **43 Alamy Stock Photo:** Travel Africa (cl); Eric Nathan (br). **Dreamstime.com:** Faunuslsd (bl). **44 Depositphotos Inc:** Meoita (cb). **Dorling Kindersley:** Blackpool Zoo, Lancashire, UK (crb). **Dreamstime.com:** Lauren Pretorius (bl). **SuperStock:** Biosphoto (cl); Roger de la Harpe / Africa (c). **45 Dorling Kindersley:** Suzanne Porter / Rough Guides (fcra). **Dreamstime.com:** Clickit (c); Ecophoto (tr); Rixie (cra); Mark De Scande (cr); Fabio Lamanna (bc). **46 Dreamstime.com:** Philip Bird (c). **iStockphoto.com:** nimu1956 (clb). **47 Alamy Stock Photo:** Images & Stories (cr). **iStockphoto.com:** misterbike (tr); vencavolrab (bc). **49 Dorling Kindersley:** ZSL Whipsnade Zoo (tr). **Dreamstime.com:** Anagram1 (tl). **SuperStock:** Juniors (br). **50 123RF.com:** Piotr Krześlak (tc). **51 Dorling Kindersley:** Hoa Luc (br). **52 Dorling Kindersley:** British Wildlife Centre, Surrey, UK (bl). **53 123RF.com:** alucard21 (tr). **Dorling Kindersley:** Rollin Verlinde (bl). **54 Dorling Kindersley:** British Wildlife Centre, Surrey, UK (bl). **iStockphoto.com:** mauribo (br). **55 Dreamstime.com:** Mikelane45 (crb). **SuperStock:** Kurt Kracher / imagebro / imageBROKER (tr). **57 Dreamstime.com:** García Juan (tr); Rosemarie Kappler (tl). **58 Dorling Kindersley:** British Wildlife Centre, Surrey, UK (cr, c); Jerry Young (cl). **Dreamstime.com:** Valentino2 (bl). **58-59 Alamy Stock Photo:** Aleksander Bolbot. **59 123RF.com:** alein (tc); Alexey Sokolov (bl). **Dorling Kindersley:** Rollin Verlinde (ftr). Fotolia: Eric Isselee (cr). **60 Alamy Stock Photo:** Danita Delimont / Gavriel Jecan (cl); Ethiopia / Panther Media GmbH (bl). **iStockphoto.com:** Danielrao (tr). **61 Alamy Stock Photo:** Art Wolfe / Cultura RM (cr). **iStockphoto.com:** fotoVoyager (tr). **62 123RF.com:** Sergey Krasnoshchokov (cl). **Dorling Kindersley:** Blackpool Zoo (bl). **63 Dreamstime.com:** Silviu Matei (tl). **iStockphoto.com:** Gerdzhikov (br). **64 Dorling Kindersley:** Twan Leenders (tr). **65 Dreamstime.com:** Dmytro Pylypenko (tl). **66 Dreamstime.com:** Rudra Narayan Mitra (bc). **67 Dorling Kindersley:** Connor Daly (tr); Wildlife Heritage Foundation, Kent, UK (b). **68 Dreamstime.com:** Vasiliy Vishnevskiy (bl). **iStockphoto.com:** Biscut (cl). **69 Dorling Kindersley:** Jerry Young (br). **70 123RF.com:** Shlomo Polonsky (bl); wrangel (br). **Alamy Stock Photo:** blickwinkel / McPHOTO / MAS (tr). **71 123RF.com:** tonarinokeroro (cra). **SuperStock:** Biosphoto (br). **72 Dreamstime.com:** Phittavas (tl). **73 123RF.com:** aquafun (tr). **74-75 Alamy Stock Photo:** David Tipling Photo Library. **74 Dreamstime.com:** Evgovorov (bl). naturepl.com: Roland Seitre (cb). **SuperStock:** Biosphoto (cra, cr); Pete Oxford / Minden Pictures (crb); Stock Connection (cl). **75 Dreamstime.com:** Mikelane45 (tc); Maxim Petrichuk (bl). **iStockphoto.com:** muha04 (cra). **SuperStock:** Biosphoto (ca). **76 Alamy Stock Photo:** David Foster (clb); Schöttger / mauritius images GmbH (cla); Frans Lanting Studio (bc). **77 Alamy Stock Photo:** WaterFrame_fba (tr). **SuperStock:** Roland Seitre / Minden Pictures (tl). **78 Alamy Stock Photo:** FLPA (br). **79 Fotolia:** Eric Isselee (br). **80 Getty Images:** Robin Bush / Oxford Scientific (bl). **81 123RF.com:** petervick167 (tl). **82 123RF.com:** Daniel Poloha (br). **Alamy Stock Photo:** Barry Brown / DanitaDelimont.com / Danita Delimont (c). **Dreamstime.com:** Izanbar (cl). **iStockphoto.com:** LeventKonuk (bl). **SuperStock:** Fred Bavendam / Minden Pictures (tr); Ron Offermans / Buiten-beeld / Minden Pictures (cr). **82-83 Alamy Stock Photo:** Norbert Probst / imageBROKER. **83 123RF.com:** antos777 (cla). **Alamy Stock Photo:** Reinhard Dirscherl (br). **Dreamstime.com:** Carol Buchanan (bc); Apidech Ninkhlai (tc); Whitcomberd (tr). **SuperStock:** Fred Bavendam / Minden Pictures (clb, ftl, tl); D. Parer & E. Parer-Cook / Minden Pictures (fbl). **84 Alamy Stock Photo:** David Osborn (bl). **85 Getty Images:** Bill Curtsinger / National Geographic (tr); David Tipling / Digital Vision (br). **86 123RF.com:** Ondřej Prosický (cla). **87 Alamy Stock Photo:** Arco / G. Lacz / Arco Images GmbH (tr). **Dorling Kindersley:** Jerry Young (br). **88** iStockphoto.com: BulentBARIS (tc). **89 Dreamstime.com:** Igor Dolgov (tr).

All other images © Dorling Kindersley

For further information see: **www.dkimages.com**